©copyright 2004, Turning Point.

"Life's like that!"

Your guide to the Lebanese

Written by: Peter Grimsditch
& Michael Karam

Illustrated by: Maya Fidawi

Introduced by: Pierre Sadek

Edited by: Nicholas Blanford

Designed by: Reem Abou Chacra

Copyright for text and illustrations:

© TURNING POINT

15TH FLOOR • THE CONCORDE BUILDING • VERDUN
BEIRUT, LEBANON
P.O.BOX 14 - 6613
TEL: 00961.1.752 100
FAX: 00961.1.748 555

FIRST EDITION: DECEMBER 2004

No part of this publication may be reproduced or transmitted in any form or by any means without the prior written permission of the publisher.

The characters appearing in this book are purely fictitious and any similarity or resemblance to any existing personalities is purely coincidental.

ISBN: 9953-0-0019-0

PRINTING: DAR EL-KOTOB

Intro by Pierre Sadek

* With all modesty, I am the world...
   ... and the world is me!

For the few of you who don't know, PIERRE SADEK is Lebanon's most respected political cartoonist. His acerbic sketches in An-Nahar newspaper and Future Television have ensured that satire is alive and well in Lebanese daily life.

بكل تواضع ..
أنا كل العالم
وكل العالم أنا ! *

About us...

British-born PETER GRIMSDITCH has been a professional journalist all his life on national newspapers in the UK and US. Editor of the Lebanon Daily Star since 1984, Middle East correspondent of the London Daily Express and a freelance writer, he counts Beirut as home. A devotee of *sawda nayyeh* (raw liver) and *arak* for breakfast, he spends a lot of time aboard his boat writing his second book, *The Uncivil War*, Untold stories of the Lebanese conflict.

MICHAEL KARAM is a journalist living in Beirut. Born in London to Lebanese parents, he returned to Lebanon in 1992, where, like the *Nightclub Dancer*, he got the shock of his life. Still, he has learned to live with most people; he is just worried that most people can't live with him.

A Fine Art graduate, MAYA FIDAWI has been illustrating since, "I can't even remember. To be honest, I have always pictured myself as a struggling artist and guess what? Here I am struggling, rather like the *Artist* in the book, who reminds me of *moi* when I was at college, only she is anorexic."

Graphic designer REEM ABOU CHACRA toiled away in ad agencies and publishing houses before finding her true calling in book design. A profound admirer of our *Plastic Surgery Addict*, Reem wishes she had the guts to have a nose job, but she is afraid her new nose will melt and fall off.

Enjoy...

Arguileh Smoker

Arguileh smoker is a serious sort of chap. He is a government employee, and therefore by nature a man who knows what he wants in life; and that is a good honest smoke. While soccer fans may argue the merits of *Ansar* over *Nijmeh*, he devotes serious time to the seemingly endless debate over what is the best tobacco: *m'aasal* or *ajami*? In fact he despises devotees of the former. They are nothing more than faddists, lightweight smokers, swept up by the recent trend for *aragueel*. The tourists have made the arguileh as common as a hamburger. And as for those plastic caps and the easy-to-light charcoal, well that just proves his point. He learned to smoke at the age of six when his grandfather the village *abaday* or hard man, gave him his first puff. That time he nearly fainted but by the time he was ten he had the lungs of a man of 50. These days, he and his fellow smokers often take their families for roadside picnics where they unpack their luxury arguileh travel kits made by Mansour of Aleppo. On these occasions they find true contentment as their wives cook *mishweh*. But if the truth were told, there are few times in life that are not arguileh time. He has been known, spontaneously to spark up on the corniche on a Sunday afternoon and even during working hours at the ministry, where his job, which involves pointing people in the direction of the photocopier, is ideally suited to his favorite pastime.

The Widow

The Widow has found a new role in life since her husband died. Previously she had been exiled to the kitchen after the birth of her last child 20 years ago, with instructions to perfect such epic Lebanese dishes as *Kousa mahshee, mouloukhieh* and *Laban Imu*. She gained 20 kilos in the process. Still her husband, *Allah yurhamu*, was a hungry man and not just for food, but then again aren't all men? She still watches the news, but has a way of interpreting politics according to who she likes, hence that nice MP from Tripoli can do no wrong. He is a nice man, a family man. Family is so important. Family and god. God has become more of a fixture the older she gets. Well he would, wouldn't he? She always says. "You never know when we will go," she always intones. To stave off the dreaded day, she sleeps at 9pm and rises at 4am. *Nem bakeer, qoum bakeer. Shoof il soha, keef betseer!* Quite. These days she wears black. Well a woman of her age should show that she has achieved something. The only other time she exerts herself is during the fits of effusion she displays whenever her youngest grandchild, Maya enters the room, at which point she throws off all decorum and begins babbling like a lunatic hen, pinching the poor baby's bottom and blowing noisy kisses on her stomach.

University Student

University student is really lost. Dragged kicking and screaming back to Lebanon by his parents, he finds that Ras Beirut does not really gel with his LA upbringing and vice versa. Through no fault of his own he is to all intents and purposes an American teen. He has a tattoo, a goatee and listens to music his live-in Teta finds hard to fathom. Because he speaks Arabic, his 'friends' call him a fraud, but he can't help it; this is how he is. He had the same problem in LA where his friends called him a "dune coon", which was a bit rich as they were all from weird countries as well. He will never be a snug fit anywhere. Currently a student at AUB, where he is studying something called Business, he just wants to play in a band with his equally confused friends, who are given equally baffled looks on campus. His dad will not hear of a career in music. He tells him he should go into marketing (whatever that is). And another thing: The tenants in his building complain when he plays his guitar on a Sunday afternoon. What do they know? They are so uncool. He recently read about this American kid who whacked his entire family because no one understood him. He can really identify with him, although he would feel bad about blowing away his sister, who is dating this freakoid who owns a restaurant in the downtown and his Teta, even though it would mean no more having to help with topping and tailing the *bemyeh*.

Plastic Surgery Addict

Plastic surgery addict believes that as Lebanese ladies have a genetic predisposition to funny noses and excessive hair, cosmetic procedures are not only a right but a necessity. Well that's what they said on Oprah. Maya couldn't wait to start and was so happy when her doctor said that she had finally stopped growing. Thank heavens! Could her nose get any bigger? Anyway she showed the doctor a photo of Uma Thurman and said she wanted that nose. Silly man tried to tell her that her face was the wrong shape. What did he know? If she had been born Swedish, she wouldn't have looked like she did in the first place and so she was only doing what nature should have done. That's what the cute sales guy at Virgin said. He was the one that told her she looked like an Arabic Uma Thurman. Well as Uma is not Arabic then she should correct this horrid flaw in nature. Anyway, all her friends love it. Then there was the problem with her moustache. Bleach it her mother said. Bleach indeed! She wasn't someone who had just come down from the village. No she had to have the electrolysis thingy. And while he was at it, he did her lower back and her tummy. *Ma maa'oul!* Where in her gene pool did it all come from?

The future? It is early days yet but she will have liposuction and she may have botox and maybe even a lip-liner tatooage. Life is such fun when you can change things. Her boyfriend Mazen has a nasty patch of hair on the back of his neck and she is trying to coerce him into getting rid of it. He thinks she is weird, but she is never going to marry him looking like that. Still he is not as bad as the guy at the gym with the chest hair that joins his beard. *Yaa!* His poor wife.

Mini Market Owner

Marwan (Abu Nader) had lived in Poland during the 1980s and seen how neglectful and unfriendly shop assistants were. Okay, there were too many per shop (to keep unemployment figures down) and little to sell anyway. When he opened up back home, it would be so different. He'd also avoid following customers round because he knew people hated that as much as being ignored.

Everyone who entered received a cheery hello and a "just ask if you don't find what you want". His business strategy was never to say no. Although most of the items were either food or small domestic hardware, he expanded to take in dry cleaning. As soon as the customer left, he would send his errand boy Mohammed to a nearby dry cleaner. The same practice applied to shoe repairs, ski sharpening, in fact all the businesses for two streets in any direction. Marwan saw himself as a neighborhood subagent. He'd send Mohammed to collect the goods whenever he saw a "subcontracted" customer approaching. It was perfect service. Other businesses received extra custom. He added 10 percent to the bills. And the customers were saved walking the streets. The service even extended to buying cigarettes if he was out of a brand and reselling it for the same price. The important thing was to get the customers coming back.

Every square centimeter of his tiny shop was packed with such a variety that only Marwan knew where everything was. And the service had to be swift as well. If more than three customers entered at the same time, Marwan stood on the sidewalk...

Grandfather (Jiddu)

Grandfather (Jiddu) is grumpy and opinionated, but he believes he has earned it and he intends to enjoy it. And why shouldn't he? His two daughters have married idiots and his son, who lives in Montreal and who is a dentist, will never amount to much. He loves his grandchildren though. He can give them back when he gets tired. He must think of his back, after all, (and his prostate, heart, knees and blood pressure while he is at it). Ah yes, in retirement he can now spend his time attending to the more enjoyable things in life, like taking his new car to the garage every time he hears a squeak (he never had time for that before) and bemoaning the state of the country and those who run it (something he always had time for). It wasn't easy at first. When he sold the factory, he was at a loss with what to do, but he has created a new routine. He has breakfast (*laban*), reads the paper (the crossword helps him forget the state of the country) plays *tawleh* with his neighbor, the retired minister (who cheats) and then comes home for lunch. After his siesta, the grandchildren visit and this reduces his blood pressure, just in time for the highpoint of the day, the news, which he watches, reinforced with several glasses of *arak*. His wife can't understand how he keeps on switching political allegiance, but he just waves his hand and tells her to pay no attention, reminding her that she never liked politics when they married, so why should she start now. Sometimes his son calls long distance while he is watching the news. Why did he bother?

Car Park Attendant

Charbel's entrée into a car park career started with a piece of personal initiative. He spotted that a daytime lot was not chained up after the 6pm closing time and so he borrowed it until the early hours of the morning. I mean, otherwise, what a waste! It saved all these diners from hunting for an empty space on the street and provided a tidy income. And how else could he get to practice Grand Prix starts over 40 feet in a $70,000 car? But in a land famed for its service, it was the little extras that furnished the icing on the cake. The introduction of a 10 percent Value Added Tax naturally required him to add LL250 to the fee. OK, 10 percent was LL150 (not that it was applicable anyway) but who's going to argue about LL100, especially if the girlfriend is in tow. And a cheery "enjoy your evening" usually avoided having to give any change at all from LL2,000.

Cramming as many cars as possible into a tight space meant parking them four deep so Charbel co-opted his two younger brothers as assistants. They soon became experts at car park solitaire, shuffling the vehicles at high speed to liberate imprisoned BMWs. André was only 12 and couldn't see over the steering wheel but he soon learned to stop hitting the neighboring cars. And 16-year-old Michel's role was a masterstroke. If diners called from their restaurant he would deliver their car to the door. The tips often doubled and sometimes trebled their income.

Society Couple

Society couple are seasoned entertainers. She hosts a party every two weeks in the hope that her name will be forever etched in Dior lipstick in the annals of Beirut society. She knows all the photographers from *Unique, Extraordinaire, Exceptionnel* and *Phenomenal*, whom she tips handsomely to ensure that she and her guests will be presented to the world in full cellulite, oops, celluloid glory. For a biggie, she can spend two months deciding what to wear. Should it be the little Gucci number or the trouser suit from Dolce and Gabbana? Maybe Elite will do a profile on her family. She can see the photo-captions now. "Family shots in the 'tasteful' salon and the 'spacious' balcony with the 'calm' Beirut smog in the distance, which she is convinced will hide any traces of the disastrous facelift she had done by the useless but gorgeous Russian surgeon with whom she had a dalliance. Her husband has a drink problem. Well who can blame him being married to her? All he gets nowadays is "but the minister's wife uses this decorator" and "the minister's wife wears this label". And there are the caterers: his wife is spending a fortune. Fortunately, she doesn't know about the twelve containers of DVDs from Azerbaijan that were confiscated or the twelve trucks that were hijacked on the road to Baghdad. He could be on the road to ruin and she's throwing parties for 300 of her closest friends, serving barbecued koala bear ears and dried sparrow lungs stuffed with rice from *Fancies* of Verdun.

Receptionist

Rita volunteered for the 2pm-10pm shift on the reception desk at her 55-room hotel. It had several advantages. She didn't have to be up too early after a night-out partying and in the low-season there was not a lot to do apart from having long, if occasionally interrupted, telephone conversations with the handsome Italian chef Alessandro.
Yet on those occasions when hotel guests did need help, she was knowledgeable, quick to help and adept in securing them the best deal on car rentals, taxis, tours or tickets. Nor was she directing them to her friends and family for a commission. Rita preferred to rely on her engaging smile, a wisp of blonde hair partly covering one eye and a slightly too tight blouse to obtain tips from the guests.
The general manager was delighted. She did her job efficiently, got on well with the customers and he had a Christmas bonus in mind for her.
To ease the boredom of the times when there was almost nothing to do, Rita struck up what for her was an ideal working relationship with Fadi, who manned the night reception from 6pm-6am. Since there was rarely a need for two people at the same time in the last couple of hours of her shift, she got plenty of opportunities to conduct her conversations with Alessandro in a room where the entire floor was empty. Yes, it was a great job... until the hotel owner called round with friends one evening to show off his flagship enterprise.

Corniche Jogger

Of the two distinct categories populating the Corniche as the sun comes up over the mountains, Ghassan is proud of the side he chose. Not for him a final *Almaza* and cigarette while slouched on a bench facing the sea after a night of partying. Ghassan planned his path right after quitting smoking. A $150 pair of Nike running shoes and two distinctive bright red tracksuits were a sound investment. Besides think of the money he was saving on cigarettes. All the surplus pounds round his midriff accumulated over the years would simply fall away and soon he'd be back to the trim, athletic shape of his college days.

Equipped with the correct kit, the next step was to mark out his patch of territory and to choose the correct time. After a series of trial runs, he hit on 6.15am as ideal to start his round trip from opposite MacDonald's to the Riviera Hotel. That way he manages to wave twice to the two attractive women running the same course in the opposite direction, once on the way there and a second time on the way back. A few regular stops to grip the top rail for stretching exercises were an essential part of the fitness routine, not to mention an ideal time to get his breath back.

The first doubt set in when a month of dedication produced no change in his weight. It also didn't help his morale when he noticed some people walking faster than he was jogging. Maybe it was the chocolate, not the cigarettes, that he should have abandoned.

Academic

Academic wears tortoise shell glasses and has long, curly unkempt black hair. He favors corduroy suits and quite frankly is at a loss with modern day Lebanese society. Where's the respect? Where is the culture? Ok, he has a Ph.D but then again so does his father's secretary. He is confused when his father cruelly reminds him of this embarrassing fact as it was his father who pushed him to get the qualification in the first place. His brother, who makes matchsticks in Nigeria and has a fleet of Mercedes, is looked upon as the success in the family, while he has spent most of his adult life trying to prove there was a vibrant Venetian community in 15th century Tripoli. His brother always gets on his case whenever he comes over for holidays. It is worst when he and his father gang up on him after meals, when they are smoking their cigars and drinking that Blue Label. He can't stand the sniggering and the annoying high fives, when they think they have scored a point against him and his bookish lifestyle. Anyway he tries not to care. Next week he is going to Heidelberg where he is participating in a symposium about the life of Jacob Burkhardt. So civilized. However in Lebanon, it is only when he takes his family for walks in the rarified atmosphere of AUB that he really feels at home, even though by his own admission things have changed. Where have all the thinkers gone?

School Student

Carla was always number one in class. It was the academic stuff she wasn't keen on. But with an endless wardrobe from Prada, Gucci and Versace, she was in a class of her own. Her Canadian teacher was a fast learner. He quickly realized that if he wanted to have her continue to flash her alluring smile and walk past just close enough for him to take in the sweet smell of *Rush* by Gucci, he should never ask her questions she couldn't answer. Not that he would ever be more than a spectator. She obviously spent more in a year on clothes than he earned in a year.

At 16, Carla had it all figured. She didn't need to know how much anything cost - the driver transported not only her but also the checks and cash to pay for everything. And *baba* was delighted she was so happy in her new school that she was taking extra classes, sometimes until six or seven at night. Her glowing reports brought a smile to his face and regular half term trips to Paris and Rome in the Lear to maintain her sartorial standards.

She learned the secret formula early on. As long as the teachers always remembered that school fees paid their salaries there would never be any complaints. And regular $100 bills (supplied by the chauffeur) for papers written by the school swot Nouhad guaranteed *baba* the opportunity to boast of his brilliant and beautiful daughter. That Marc picked her up in his Cayenne five minutes after the extra-curricular history of philosophy course started and returned her ten minutes before it ended at 7pm was a secret the whole school knew but never shared.

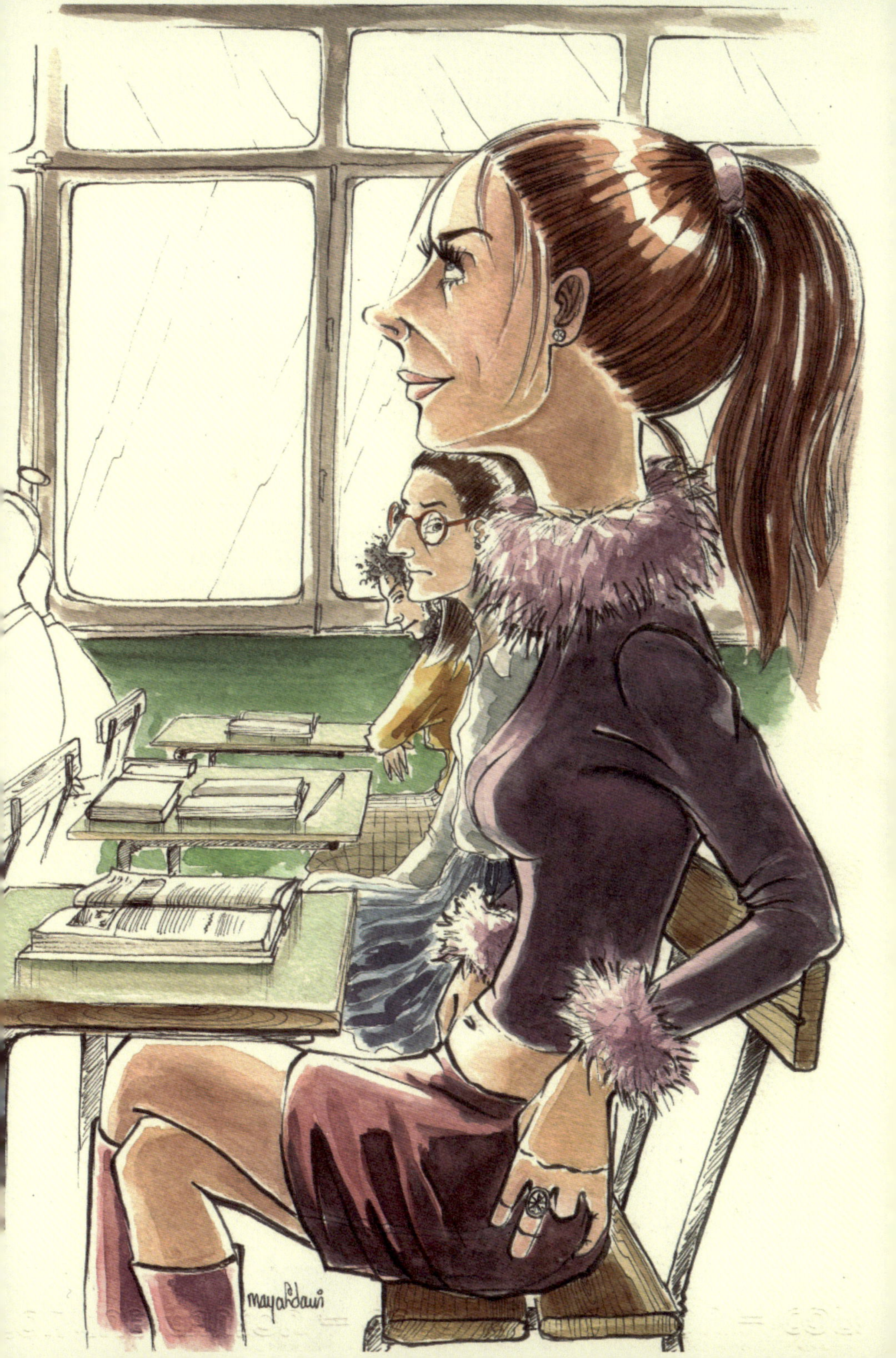

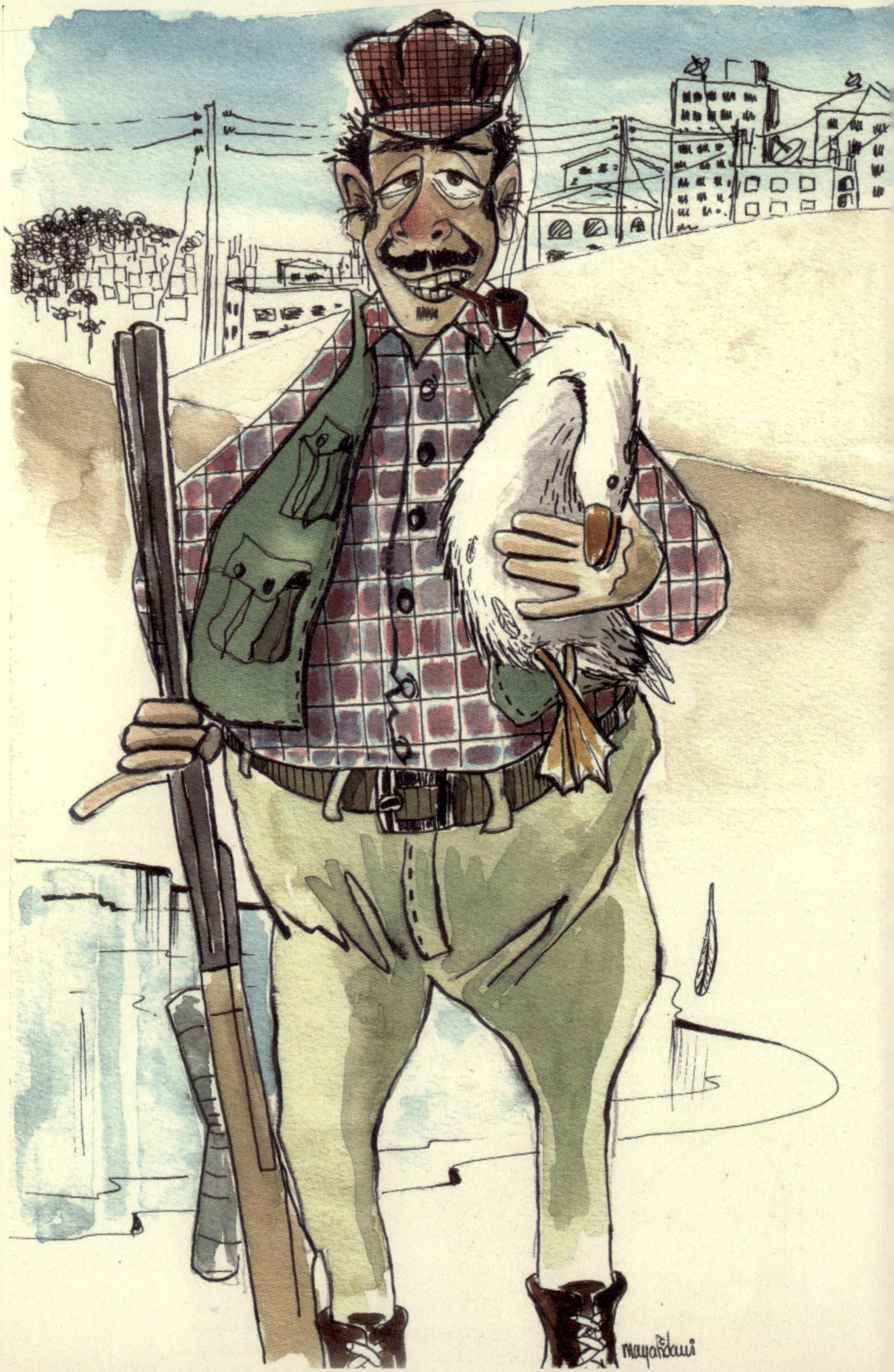

Bird Hunter

Bird Hunter just can't understand why the government banned hunting. It's such fun. Still, he's happy it is not a real ban. He can still go after anything he wants including the big migrating birds or even eagles. An eagle; now that would be something. His friend Issam shot a stork (although it did take several hits before it fell) and got an angry phone call from an environmentalist who said it was a rare bird and that he (Issam) was a hooligan. What does he know? This year, he has bought a new weapon, a Chuck Norris Autograph pump action, like one he saw in Delta Force Killers. His father told him using such a gun was cheating. But why not move with the times? He can now fire ten rounds in as many seconds, giving him a better chance of actually hitting something. Anyway, he believes he has become a more responsible hunter. There was a time when he sat on his balcony in the summer house in Broumana and shot at anything that flew. Now he makes trips to remote, unspoilt areas in his '87 BMW, where he can blissfully blast away without disturbing the neighbors, who might complain that he doesn't pick up his empty cartridges. Don't they understand that when winter comes along they will all be washed away by the rain. Still there have been mishaps. He once hit a power cable while trying to bring down a flock of geese, leaving the nearby village with no electricity for a month; he didn't go back there for a while. He is thinking of upgrading the pump action next year. An RPG - now that would be a good weapon.

Doctor

The Eastern European degrees may not have had the same cachet as the equivalents from France or Britain or the United States, but they had given Dr. Fouad more than enough letters after his name to necessitate a slightly oversize name plaque outside his clinic. Well, maybe clinic was slightly too grand a term. His part of the two-room suite had his desk, three chairs, an indoor plant that seemed more in need of attention than some of his patients and an elderly examining couch covered with a paper sheet. The entrance led into the other room where sat his cousin Madonna, who acted as appointments clerk, receptionist and, most importantly, cashier.

His specialty had become knees and elbows; not very glamorous but very profitable. Take that young chap who wrecked tendons in his left knee in a skiing accident. It was so swollen he couldn't straighten his leg. Clearly time for an X-ray. "Bring the results back and I'll see you next week." So $50 for a consultation and Fouad's commission on the X-ray referral. The X-ray was blurred because the knee was bent, so better have an MRI scan. Another $50 and a cut of the $350 scan fee. "We may need to operate but I'd like to avoid it if we can. Let's see what it's like in a week." Another $50. Seven days and a couple of pokes and prods later brought another professional observation: "This is not healing as quickly as I had hoped. Come and see me next week."

Many five-minute consultations and $50 bills later, Mother Nature achieved a cure without the benefit of medical qualifications.

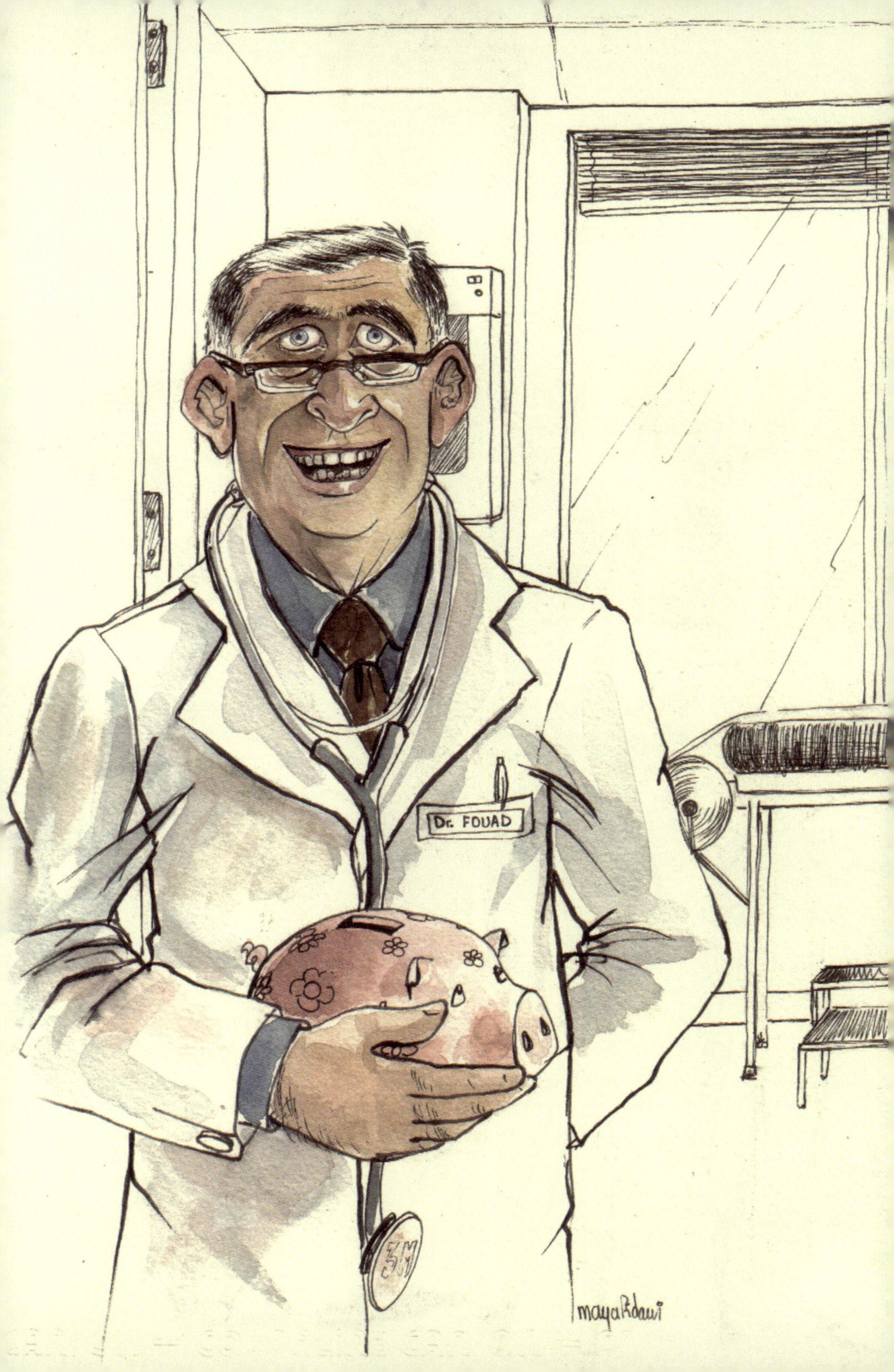

Dr. FOUAD
mayaRdawi

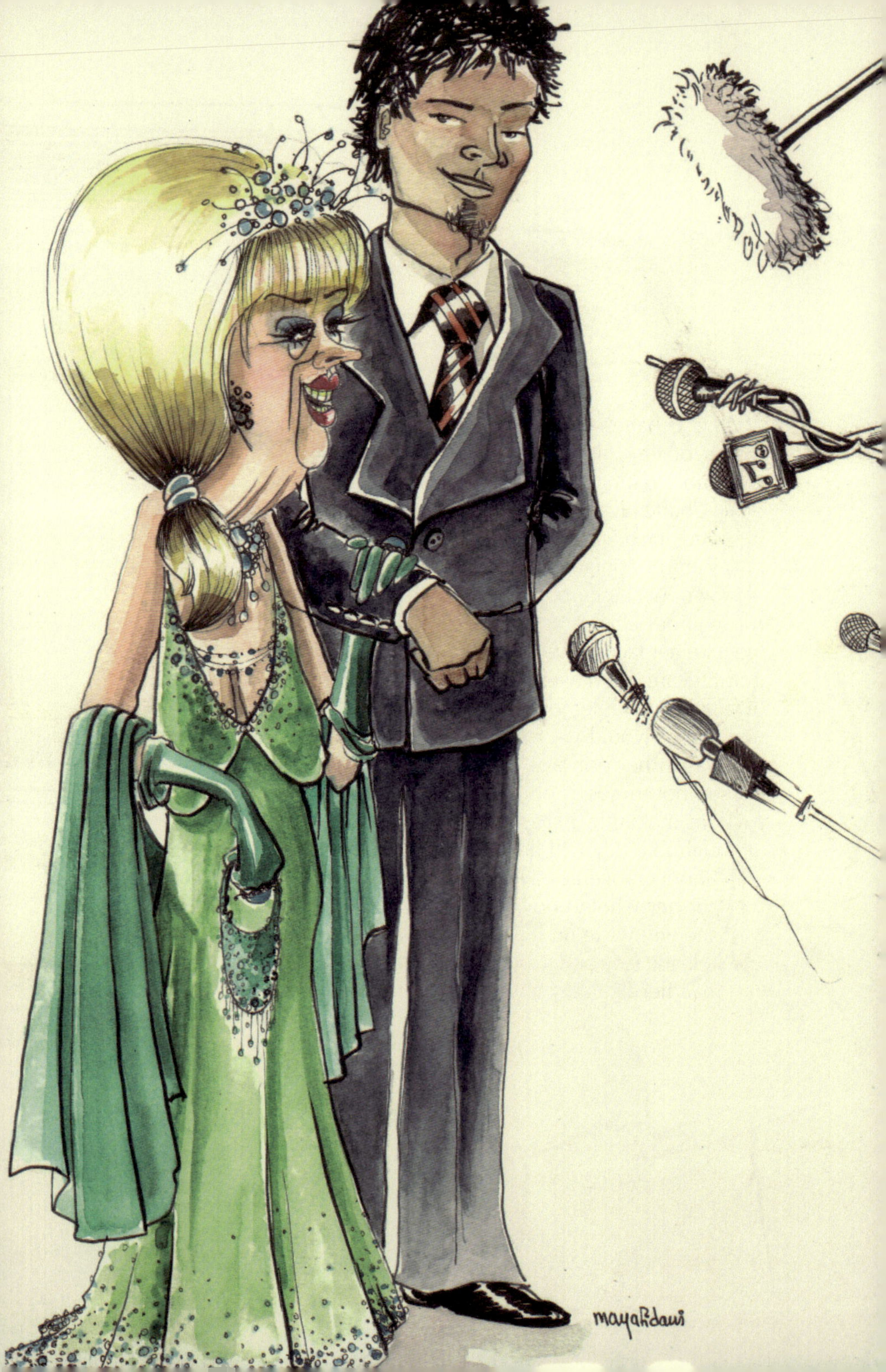

Ageing Lebanese Singer

Ageing Lebanese singer has worked hard at arresting the march of time. It isn't easy looking 35 when you can still remember dating a French mandate officer and you look on dear Charles Aznavour as a toy boy. She is now on her 12th husband. Hadi is 25 and also acts as her manager (as they always did). Tonight he is taking her to dinner. She loves the feeling of walking into the restaurant and feeling the frisson of recognition, although the glare of the lights often makes her feel like her face is melting. Yes Hadi is much younger but she doesn't care. He makes her feel good and her fans don't mind. In fact they love her for it. Her fans are all she has. She is loved and where would we be without love. They knew her when she was in her prime. They grew up with her and they have chosen not to desert her, apart from the ones who have died and are making a place for her to one day sing in heaven, although that day will have to wait, especially as she has just read about cryogenics. Hadi tells her she can freeze either her head or her whole body, to be revived years into the future. Yes, she will wake up in 100 years and walk onto the stage at Baalbek and sing and sing and sing and they will cry and cheer and love her like they always did. They are her fans.

Cashpoint Man

Cashpoint man not only uses the ATM; he sets up base camp, arranging, on the slim ledge along the front of the screen, his car keys, Filofax, and cellular phone. He then searches for his credit card wallet and carefully removes his ATM card. He has been told that the screen is designed in such a way that only the user can see it, but he is not convinced. While carrying out his transaction, he will execute a well-rehearsed turn, gyrating his torso, to check that no one is watching him. Unlike most normal people who complete their transaction and move smartly off to make way for the next person, our man takes his time. He slowly goes through the whole process in reverse, putting money in wallet and card neatly back in cardholder. He will read his receipt and then tear it up. Finally he will pick up the rest of his paraphernalia and walk off into the distance leaving a queue of people that have spent the last five minutes fantasizing about roasting him over an open fire. On some days he uses several different cards at a time. Thus he will withdraw money with his ATM card; order a statement with his Bank of Bosnia credit card; transfer money with his Bulgarian Amex and finally e-mail his mother with his special Bank of Dubai smart card. He has no sense of urgency and is oblivious to the impatient foot tapping and restless sighs behind him. He is a citizen of the world; let them wait.

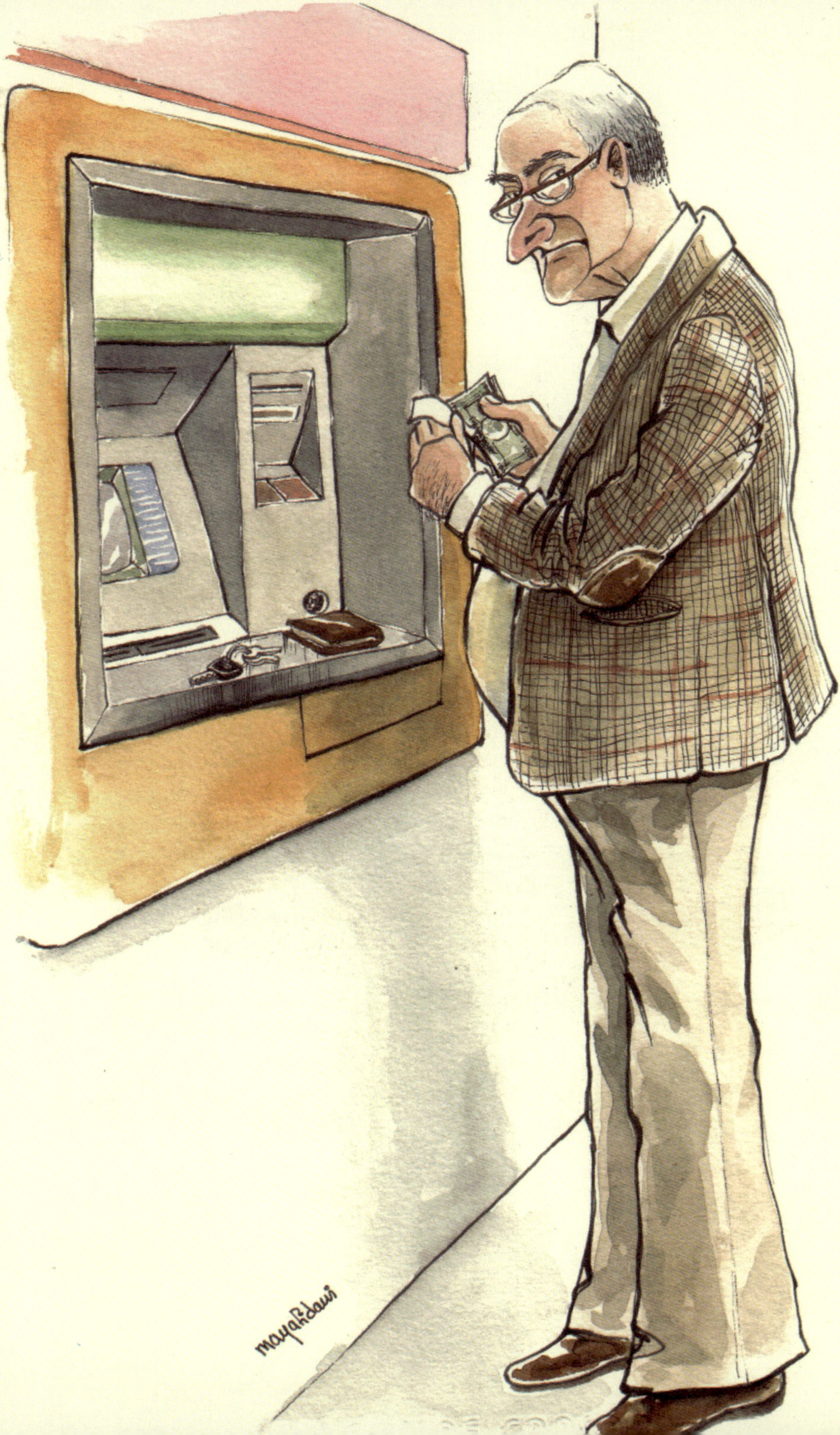

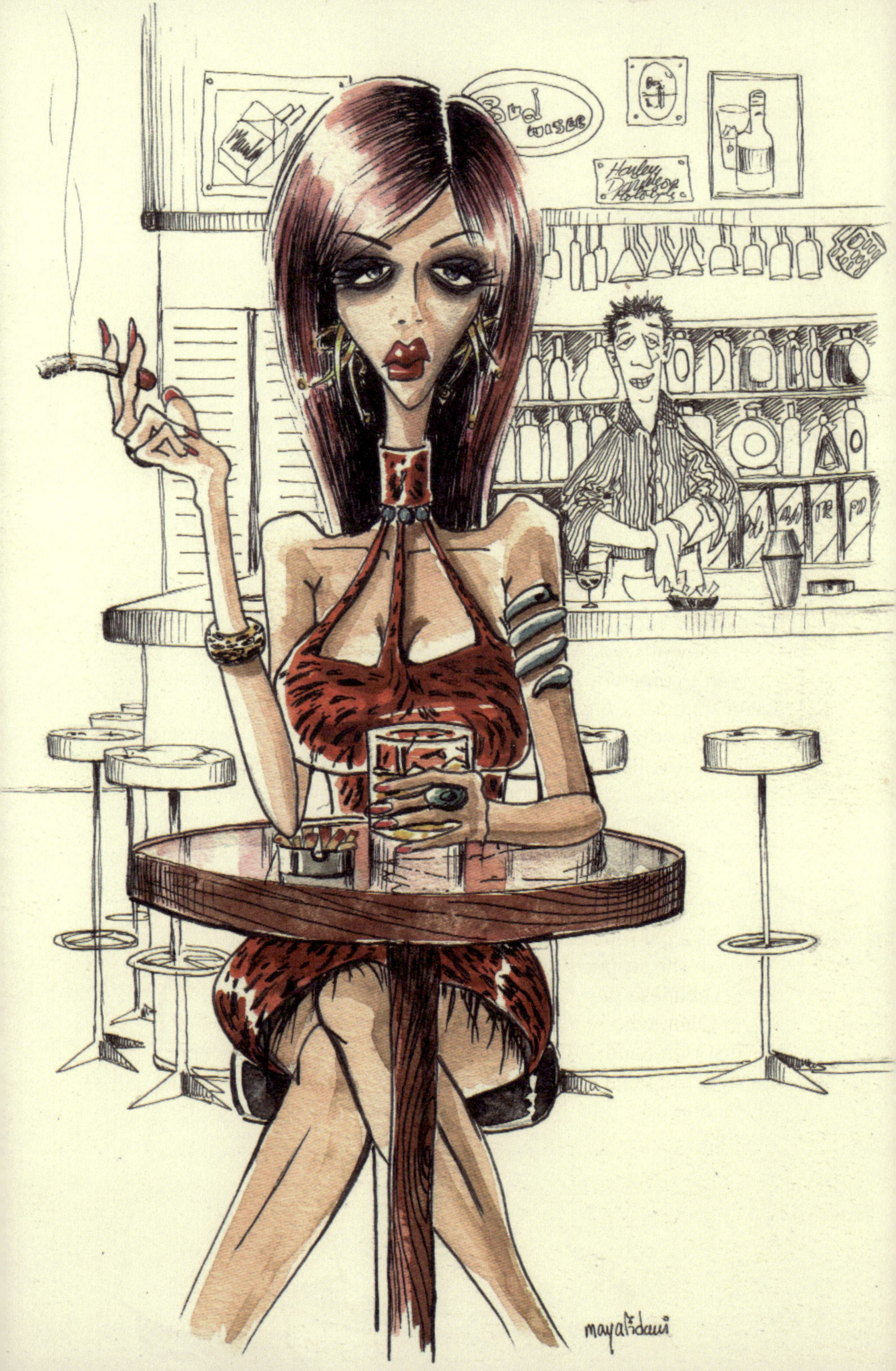
Bud
WISER

Nightclub Dancer

Nightclub dancer comes from Russia, but was taken away from all that when she met Boudi at Smolensk University. He seemed such a nice guy at the time. He told her he would get her a job in his father's business when they graduated. Did he propose? Well no, but she just assumed she would be part of this great family he kept talking about. What she didn't know was that it would be made up of 30 other Russian "sisters" living in a motel near Tabarja. Boudi soon gave up on her when they arrived. It turns out he was married all along. Still, she can't complain. He keeps an eye on her and makes sure the customers at *Big Stallion*, his father's super nightclub don't get too friendly. Can she dance? Well that's another thing. She had to learn all that to be part of the floorshow. This week she was a member of the world famous Cosmonauts, direct from Moscow. For one week only! Surely the regulars would realize that last week she was part of the equally famous Cossacks and one of the Zhivago Girls the week before that. Oh well, at least she has a boyfriend, Fadi, a cousin of Boudi, who has a car lot in Zouk and who wants to make her happy, although she suspects he might be married too. What is it with these Lebanese guys? Don't their wives look after them? Her friend Olga, who really is a Cossack, tells her to hook up with the first rich Saudi guy to come along, like she has. Yes he is married, but Olga says it is okay because they can have lots of wives. She asks if he has proposed. She said no. She must be careful.

High Flyer

High Flyer left Lebanon, went to Harvard and Oxford (or was it Oxford and Harvard), returned, and now earns $150,000 working for a vast multinational. He got his doctorate in philosophy, but knew that the tweedy, threadbare life of an academic wasn't for him and certainly was a "no no" in the intellectual vacuum that is Lebanon. So he is now reaping the rewards for having waded through Neitzche. His apartment however, is a shrine to his beloved Ivy League days. A pipe sits proudly near his favorite armchair, next to the bottle of Glen Sporran malt whisky. His fiancée, Rima, found him a bit stuffy when he first returned, but given his salary and family connections, this was nothing a bottle of Davidoff Cool Water, a jumbo Meisterstück and platinum Rolex couldn't sort out. Anyway she wasn't going to let this one slip through her fingers. Maroun finds Rima's style tips a bit annoying, even if the cologne she selected for him seems to have an extraordinary effect on her. So what if she has never read Neitzsche? The dancing however is a problem. They go out every Saturday night and Rima always ends up boogying on the table. He cant understand what has possessed her. He sits and smiles; every now and then glances at his new Rolex and twiddles with the pen in his shirt pocket while she dances with the waiter. It is at times like this he yearns for the comfort of Nietzsche.

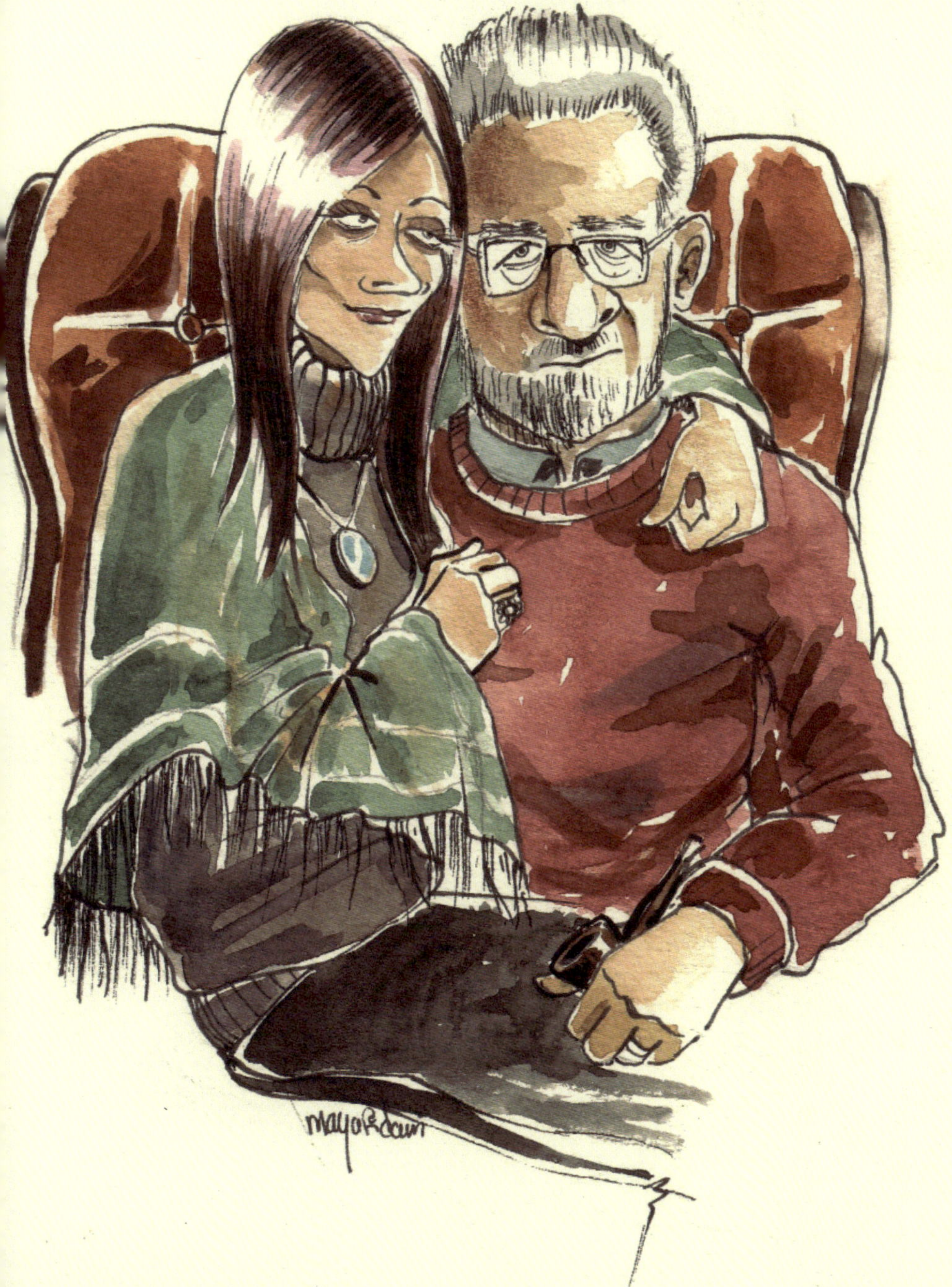

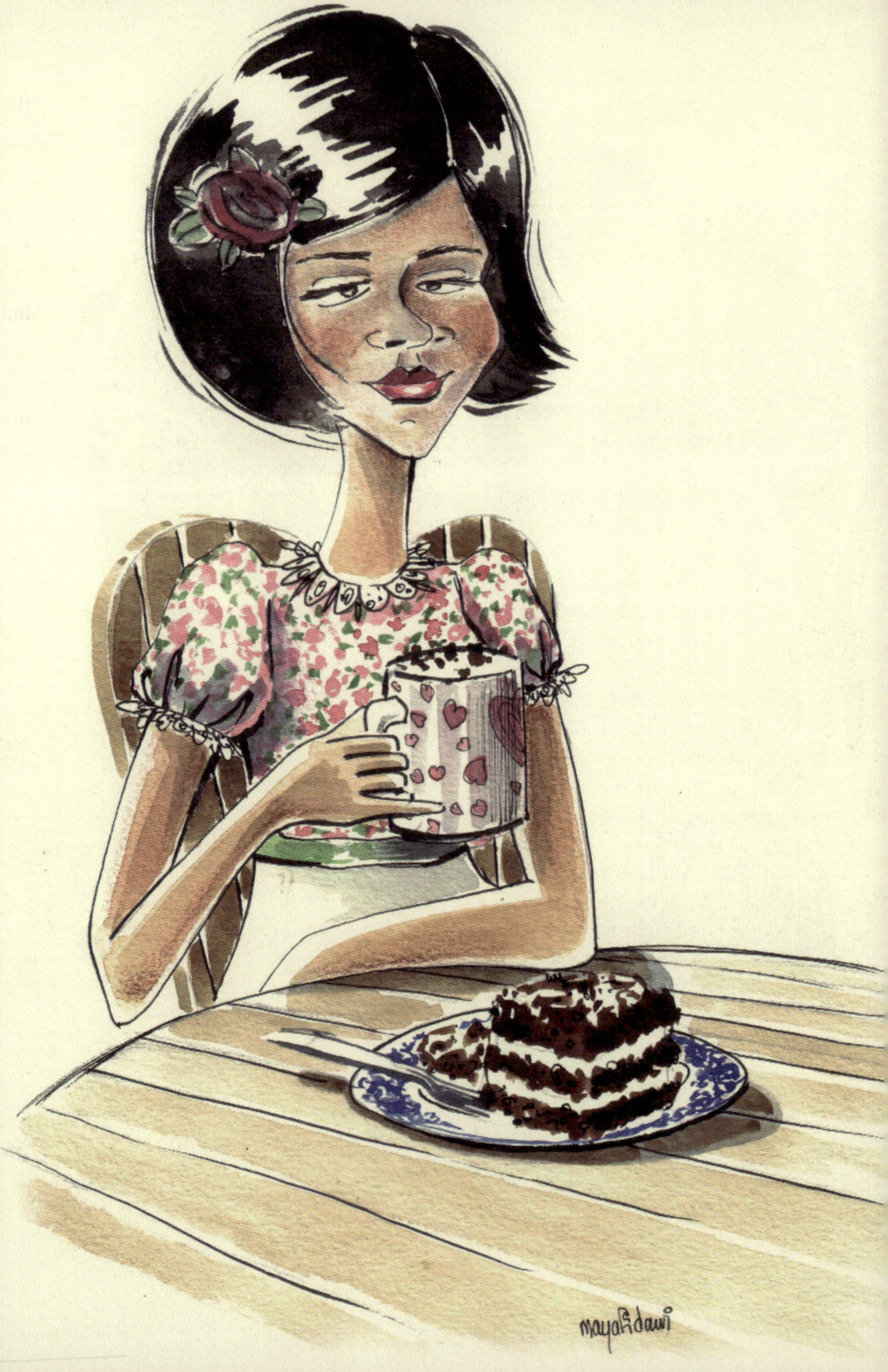

Daddy's Princess

Daddy's princess loves cappuccino with extra chocolate on the top. Leena is certain she will marry a prince because her father says she will. She is 25. But a lot of her friends tell her she acts much younger. She is not sure if that is a compliment. She is dating Kareem. She loves him but her father says his prospects are not good enough and his parents are not like them. She spends her days pretending to do an MA (but complains that reading gives her bags under her eyes). She suffers from anxiety attacks and calms down by eating chocolate fudge cake. In the summer she lives at the beach where her family has a cabin and spends her day drinking diet Pepsi and eating chef's salads. She will take over her father's company. Most important people in her life are mummy and sister and dog, Sasha, a Pekinese. Kareem lectures her about having to have goals in life. She teases him by threatening to go out with Michael who is "sooo lovely, and sooo rich, but she would never marry Mike. He is such a playboy. Still, he does drive the most delicious Mercedes, the one with the cute headlights, designed by Hermes. If Mike behaves, she might reconsider but he would have to show her he is serious by buying her the latest Vertu mobile phone. Now that would be a start. In the meantime, she will wait for the prince that daddy says will come along...one day.

Cigar Puffing Businessman

Tarek knew he had it made. What was important was to make sure everyone else knew it too. Years of healthy commissions on construction contracts had brought the Lear, the boat and the extra properties in Europe and the Bahamas. But his prize possession was the Cohibas specially flown in from Havana for his consumption. That put him alongside presidents and kings. He lodged a box at his favorite restaurant, which thoughtfully supplied cut-glass ashtrays with "Cohiba" engraved on the bottom. Keeping the label on the cigar as he puffed away over lunch was an even more effective advertisement for Tarek's importance.

His favorite bit of one-upmanship was to persuade a fellow diner to take one of his personal imports (having first ensured he knew nothing about cigars). Then, after smelling and lightly squeezing his own, he would loudly announce they couldn't smoke them because they weren't fresh. A phone call and his driver would deliver a new box.

It had never really mattered to Tarek if all the other people at the table were still eating when he wanted to indulge. Once extravagantly lit with a match that almost matched the cigar's own length, his Cohiba would send a billowing cloud of expensive smoke down the table. It was effective enough to convert all salmon dishes into *saumon fumé*.

But truth will out and it was a little thing that gave him away. He couldn't break the habit of flicking the ash as though he had a Marlboro Light in his hand.

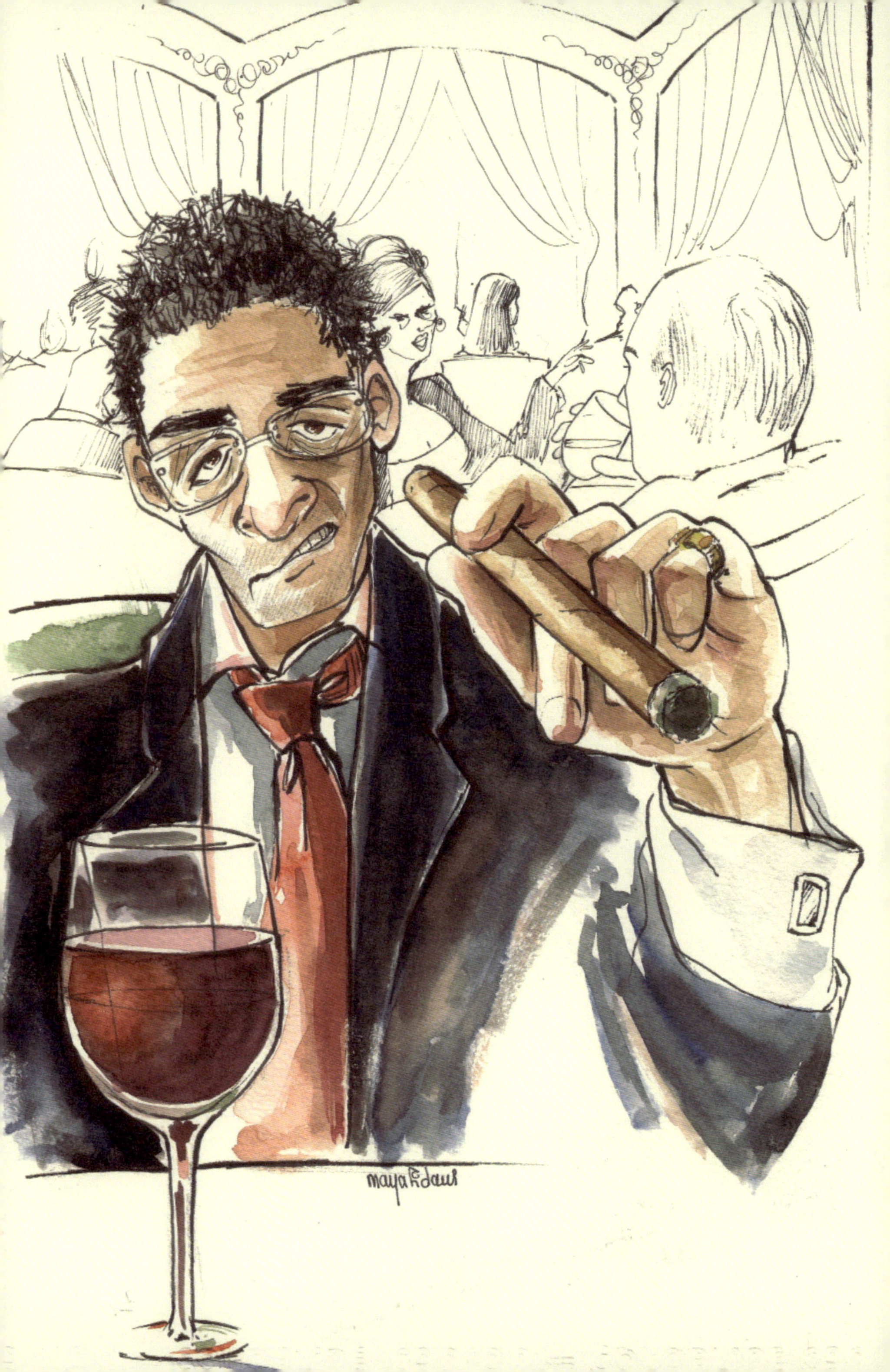

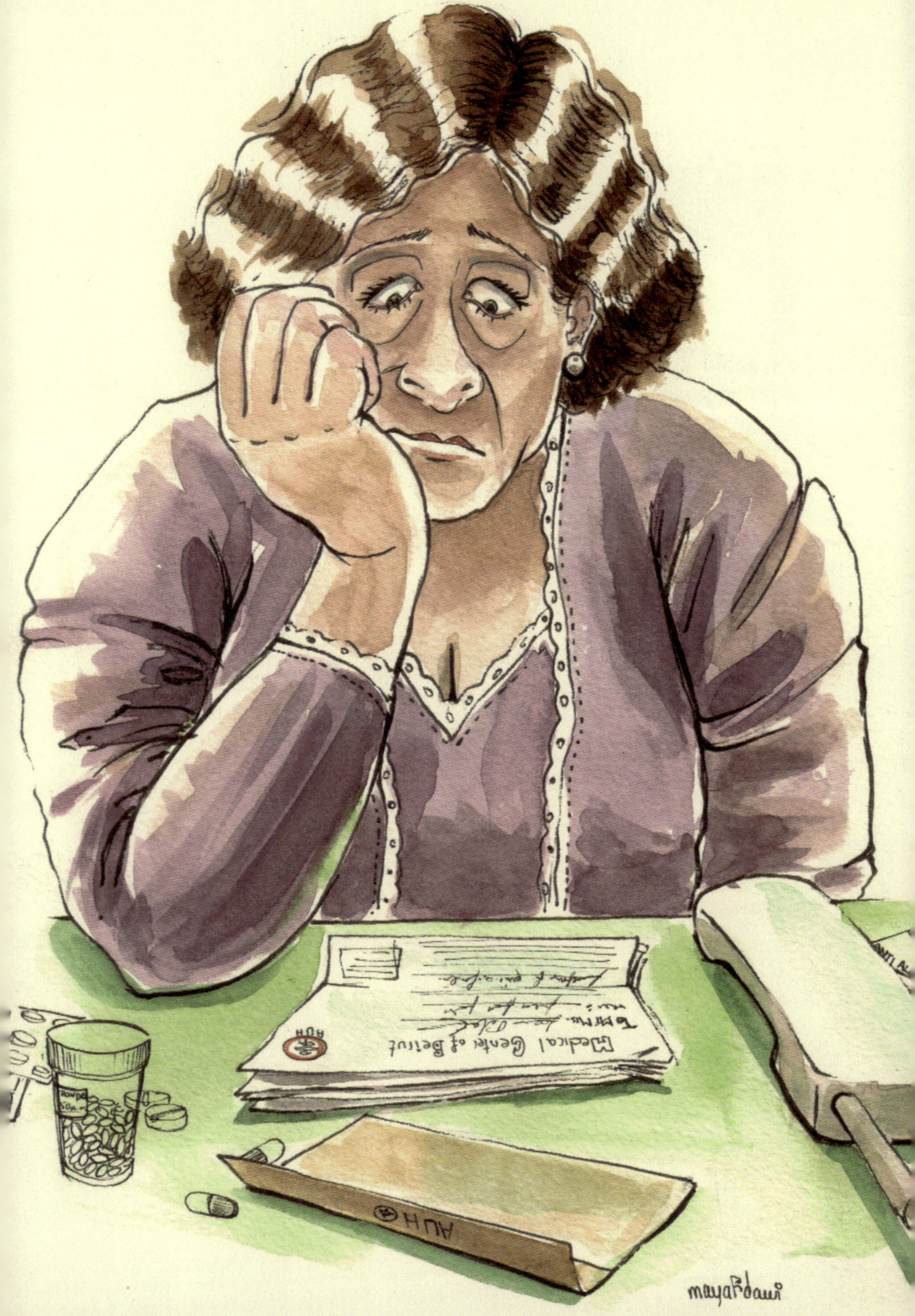
Medical Center of Beirut
AUH

Hypochondriac

Divorced and lonely, Aida realized the root cause of her problems after watching a medical research special on the Discovery Channel. She was seriously ill. That's why her ex had lost interest in her. Though friends had kept her in their circle when Hamoud shot off to the Gulf with his floozie new bride, she was always the odd one out at a dinner party. Other women talked of their husbands and children. Aida tried to avoid mention of the man who had run out on her and the two boys, grown up now, had moved on to Seattle and Milan. But these were friends so she could confide her health problems. The effect was stunning. Suddenly she was the center of attention and sympathy. Aida too had something to talk about. She even shared the 14-page results of her latest blood tests and the MRI scan over morning coffee. They were impressed though equally clueless about what all the numbers meant.
Liban Telecom's income soared as her three sisters, also scattered round the world, were regularly updated by telephone on her various illnesses. And Dr. Ajami's practice was also benefiting as he prescribed a variety of harmless drugs before she paid the $50 consultation fee on her way out. After all, he reasoned, it was cheaper for her than seeing a psychiatrist. Aida told him the problems might be hereditary because Aunt Zeinab had complained of similar symptoms. In fact, she was also the one who urged Aida to read up as much as she could on medicine.

Turneeb Team

Turneeb team is typically made up of two atypical players: Partner A is terrible and never remembers the cards that have been played, thus conspiring to demolish any strategy Partner B, his best friend, may have planned. The game is therefore punctuated by aneurysm-inducing screams from B as A wastes yet another high card even though the trick has been won. This caused much wailing and gnashing of teeth in the previous games, when Partner B, so disgusted by his team mate, threw his cards down on the table and abandoned the table to sulk in his car (a 15-year old BMW 323i with a "Michael Schumacher" sticker stretched across the rear windscreen). His departure, albeit a display of petulance, is lethal. As all Lebanese know, it is hard enough to get four people to sit around a table at the best of times, let alone keep them there. Still, these tiresome lows are compensated by rare highs, when B plays with Zen-like cool mixed with dramatic theater and A actually concentrates. When the cards are falling favorably, B plays like a Swiss watch. He deals like Omar Shariff, rakishly arranges his cards like Paul Newman and plays like Sean Connery, carelessly lighting another Marlboro as he flicks out a succession of killer cards with a Bond-like ruthlessness. The game will progress to its thrilling denouement. The Mediterranean in him rises to the surface as he slams down the winning card with an indecent flourish and high-fives the partner he came close to murdering in the previous game.

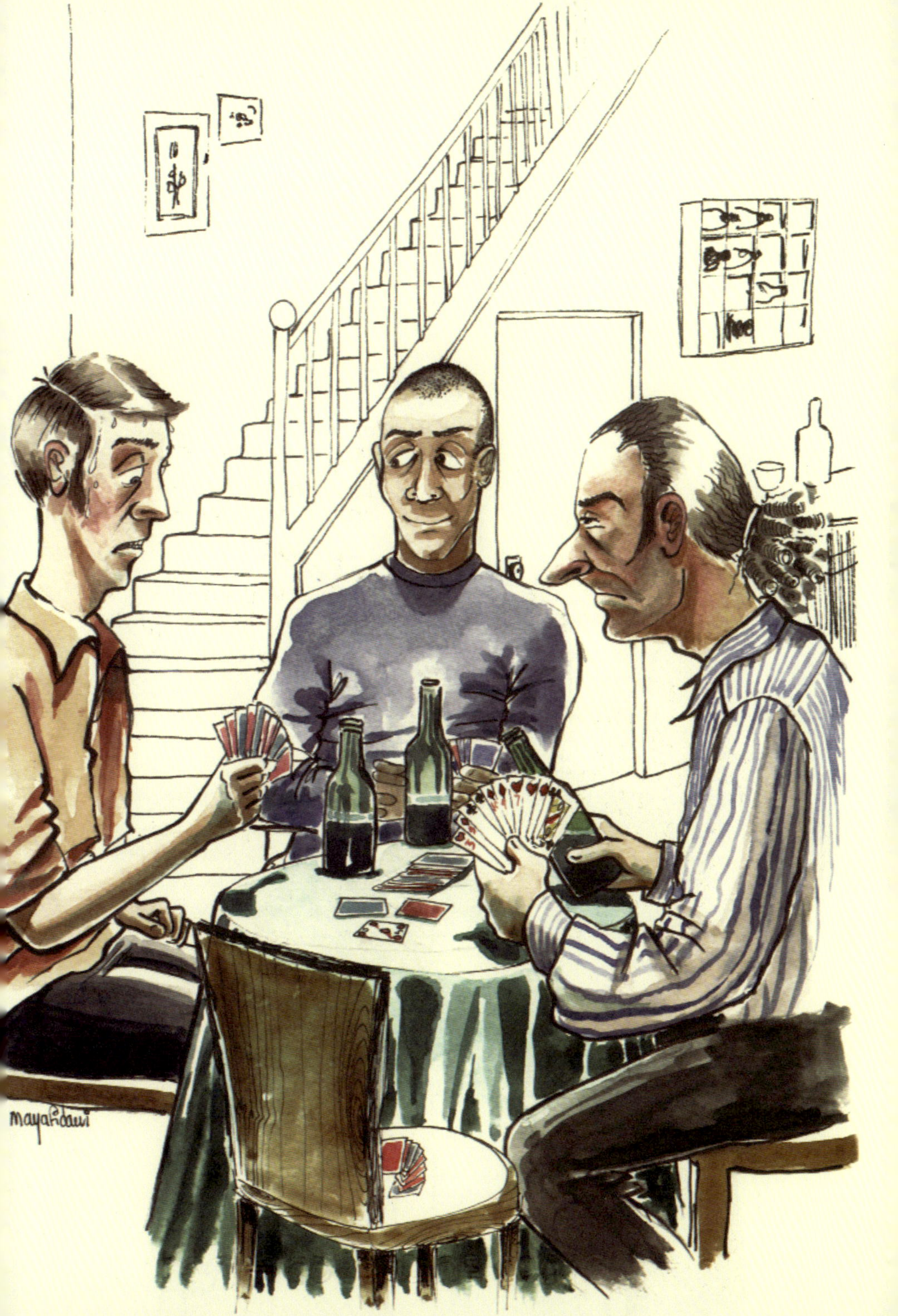

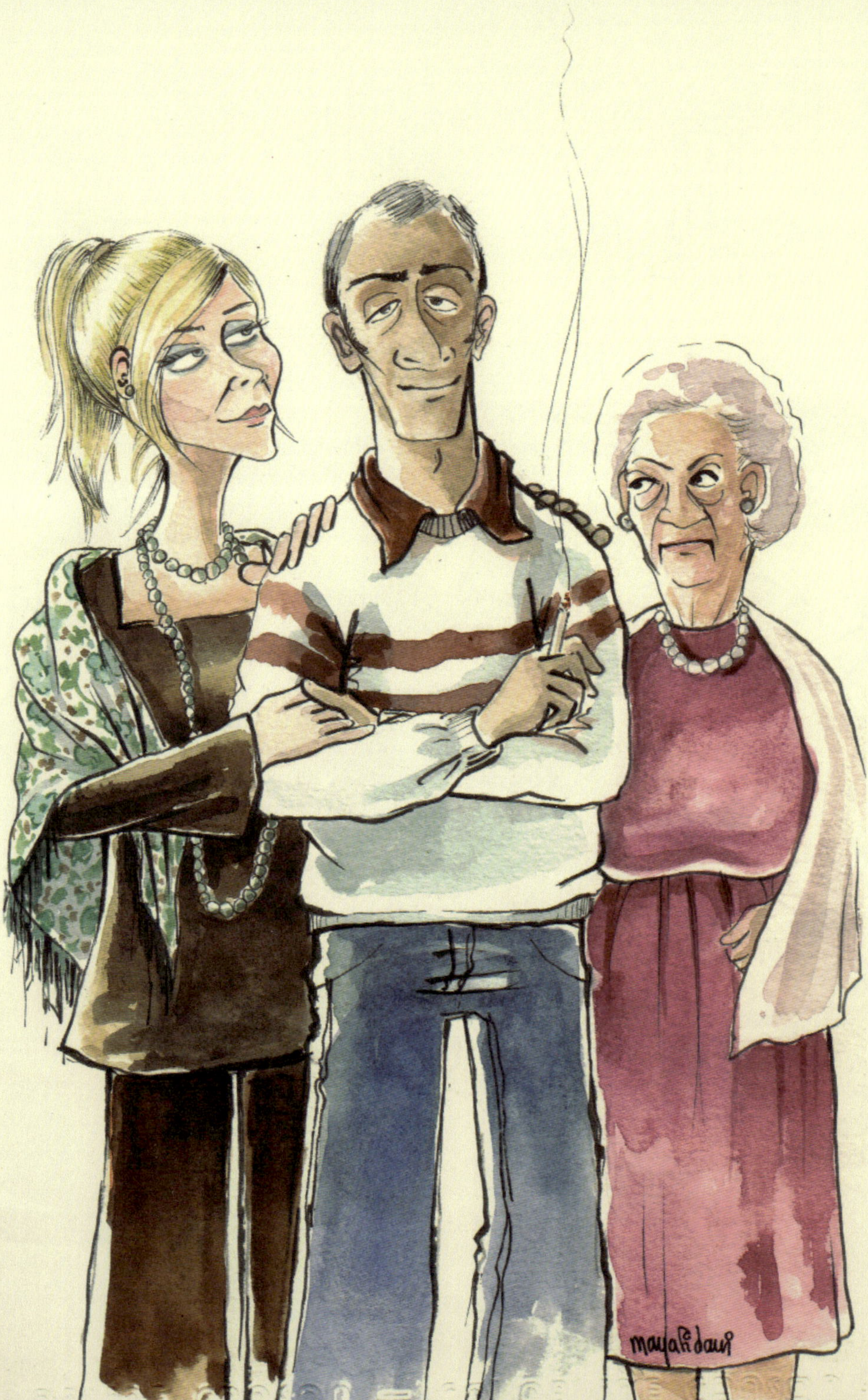

Foreign Wife on Holiday

Gloria met Farid - the Frank bit was her idea - at university in New Jersey. It hasn't been easy. Her wheelchair-bound father still distrusts Frank, keeping his Remmington pump-action shotgun handy every time Frank visits. He remembers the Achille Lauro and is convinced that Frank wants to roll him off the porch. Gloria's mother, who advised her against the marriage, is worried about her daughter being in the Middle East: "They're different to us honey" and for her time in Lebanon, has given her a hotline number at the embassy. "Remember *Not Without My Daughter* dear. You never know what these people are like, when they get back among themselves. And don't eat the food." For her part Gloria is happy to support her husband and accompany him on his trips back to what he calls "the most beautiful place on God's earth". He is decent, albeit a tad boring, and she can't say that about many of her friends' husbands. Still, the endless rounds of coffee, the incessant smoking, the questions about how often she and her husband make love and the whispers - "Only one child? *Yimkin fee mishkli*" - can get to her. Most irritating and if she were honest, disappointing, is her relationship with her mother-in-law, who heard that she had a serious boyfriend before she met Frank and therefore thinks her son should have married Salma, a virgin, from the village. But she has tried to take an interest in cooking, learn a few words of Arabic and insist that their son write to Teta every holiday (try getting Frank to do that!), but still she can't get through. Maybe they are different after all?

Civil Servant

The real measure of Ahmad's success in the ministry could be measured by the number of rubber stamps he had on his desk and the fact that he had to refill his stapler at least twice a day. With at least half a dozen people milling round his rusting gray metal desk at any given time, each clutching a bundle of papers some of which he personally had to initial he considered himself a vital cog in the bureaucratic machine.

However, life did not always run smoothly. Although he was finally mastering which stamp to use on which bit of paper, he could never quite remember where he'd put it down the last time he used it. So it took up quite a bit of his day turning the rubber stamps upside down and trying to decipher from the mirror image facing him whether it was the appropriate one.

The other problem was that there was always someone trying to obtain the permit they needed without providing all the correct documentation, with three photocopies of some and two of others. These needed also to be put in the right order, checked and rechecked.

Ahmad would have liked to serve everyone at once and often tried to do that. By perpetually switching from one client to another he was continually surrounded by people who needed his say-so. It didn't do much for productivity but he was always busy. In any case, thoroughness was more important than speed. Now if you wanted more productivity, a new stapler that didn't keep jamming as he hammered it down on 10 sheets of paper...

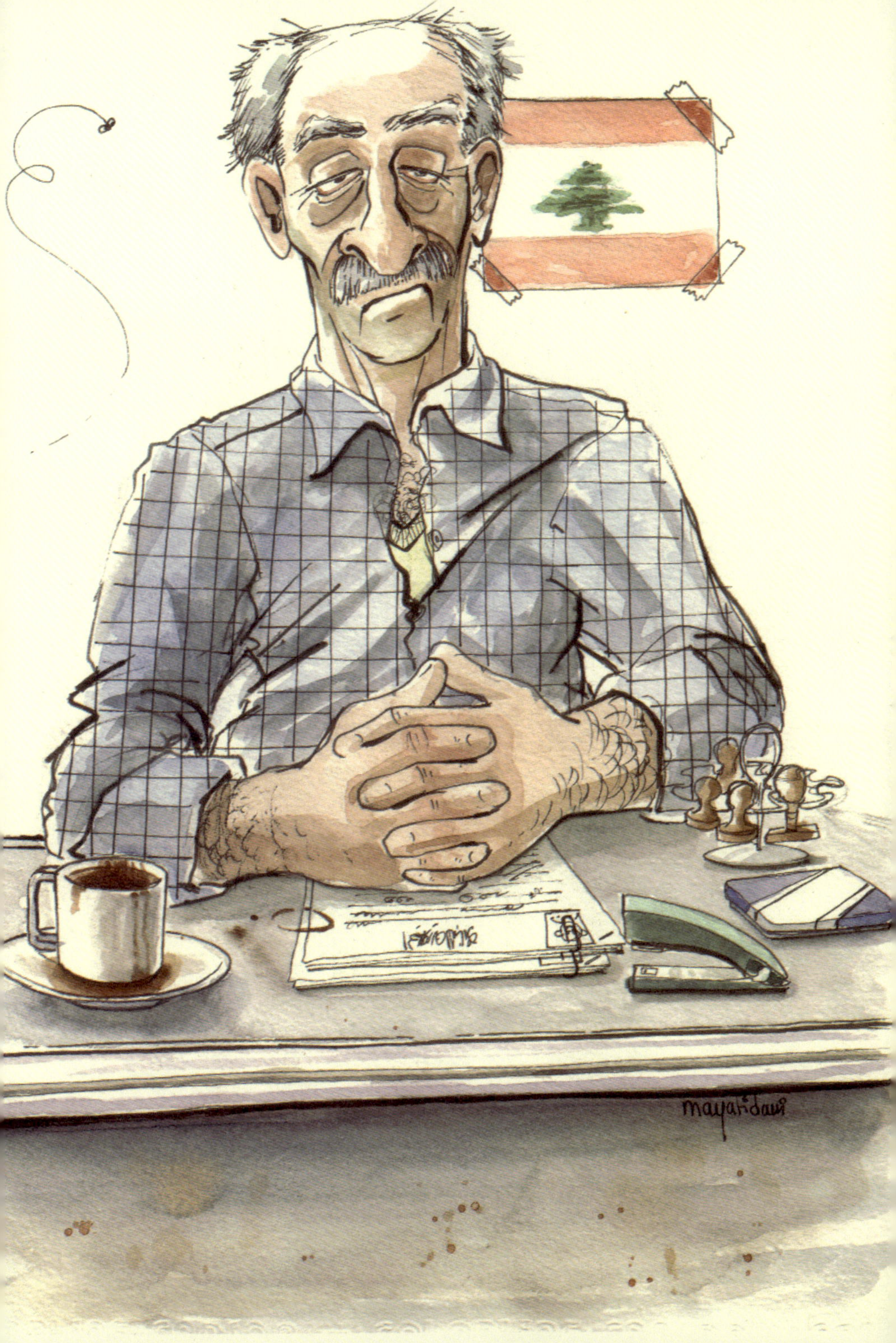

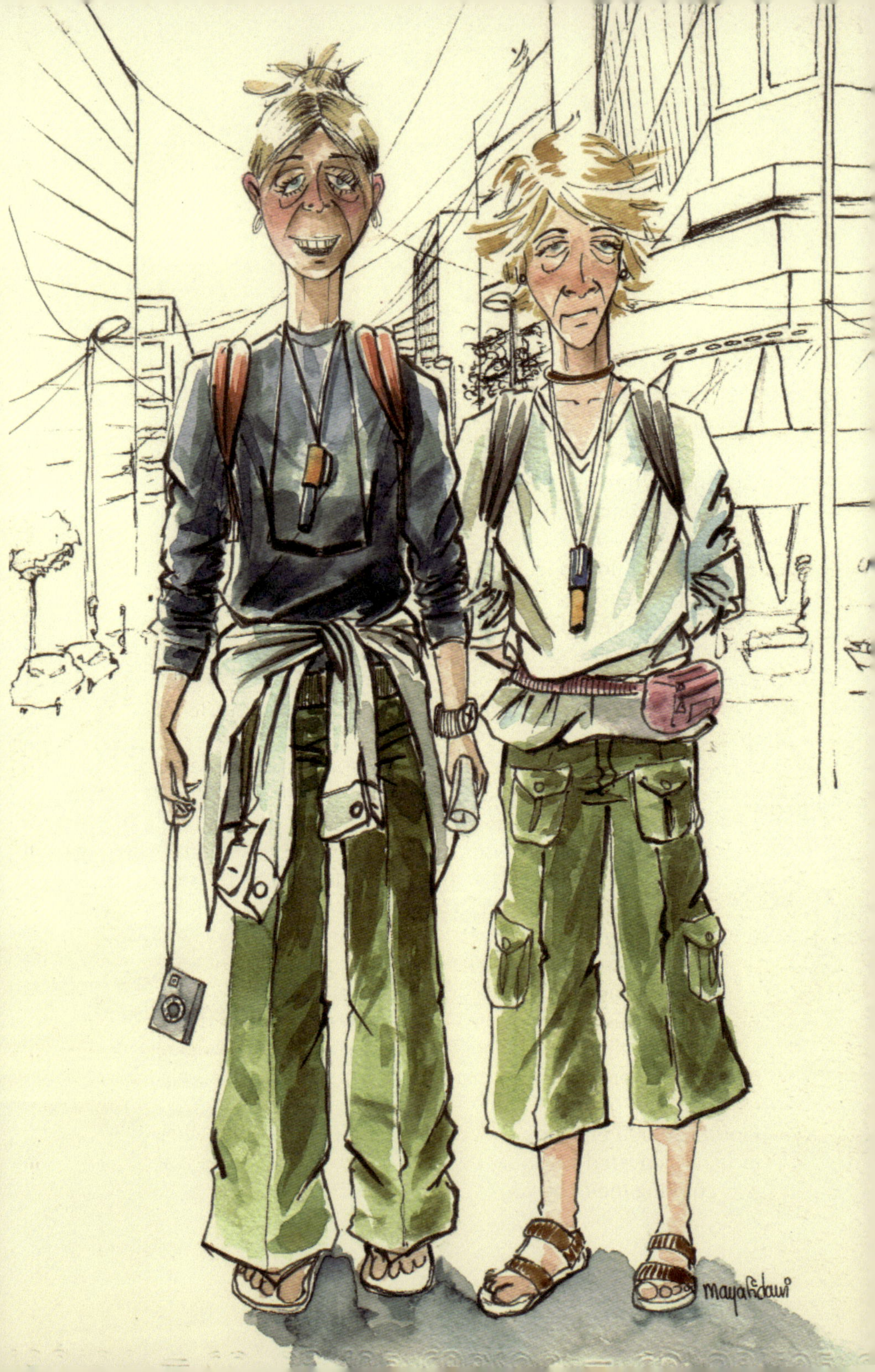
mayafidawi

Foreign Tourists

The two 40-year-old women had never been further afield from Britain than Benidorm in Spain, which, lets face it, is England in the sun. "It'll be great," Charlotte told her best friend. "I read in a magazine that Lebanon's culture goes back thousands of years." Connie was convinced and the pair left their families for the exotic adventure of a lifetime with a determination to be "sensible", especially with their clothing. It was common sense that made them rebuff an offer outside Beirut Airport of a taxi - "cheap, $20" - in favor of a cab with a meter inside. They were not totally convinced they'd done the right thing when 15 minutes later they parted with $38 for the ride to Hamra.
Still attractive, albeit with (backsides/bottoms) prone to spreading, Connie and Charlotte had bought identical khaki shorts that reached to their knees to avoid any possibility of giving offense. After all this was an ancient culture and they had to be respectful. Since they were also wearing long-sleeved baggie tops, they couldn't understand why so many drivers of battered old Mercedes were hooting their horns at them as they strolled along Hamra Street.
And the ten-minute walk along the bustling streets to the beach club was an eye-popper. While the pair broiled in the midday sun, there were bare midriffs everywhere, plunging necklines galore and skirts that seemed smaller than the belts on their new shorts. But the real shock came after they paid their LL20,000 entrance fee and came face to face with acres of barely covered reclining flesh. Now it wasn't the sun that was coloring their cheeks.

Aspiring Politician

Charif had it figured out when he was a teenager. Make a million, preferably a few, build up stacks of influential contacts and put his branch of the family back in the public spotlight where it should be. After all, his grandfather had been one of the founding pillars of the country. If only dad hadn't squandered everything on Black Label and foreign blondes. But Charif wasn't going to make the same mistakes. Twenty years of bowing and scraping in the Gulf provided the means (and lots of practice in agreeing with everything his sponsors said).

His assistant scanned the death notices so Charif could appear at the condolences of everyone related to an influential family and charity functions were ideal territory for getting his photo in the papers. Charif's trademark was the cardboard cutout smile, directly facing the camera and tucked in behind the shoulder of the most important man there. With sometimes up to four events an evening, the schedule for changing his suits between each one was as hectic as his diary itself.

Regular visits to his home town in the mountains as well as carefully calculated (and publicized) donations to worthy causes laid the groundwork for possible future election to parliament and the first big breakthrough came when a government minister asked Charif to represent him at diplomatic parties and some official functions. If only his wife could change clothes as quickly as he could - then he would be able to fit in even more public appearances.

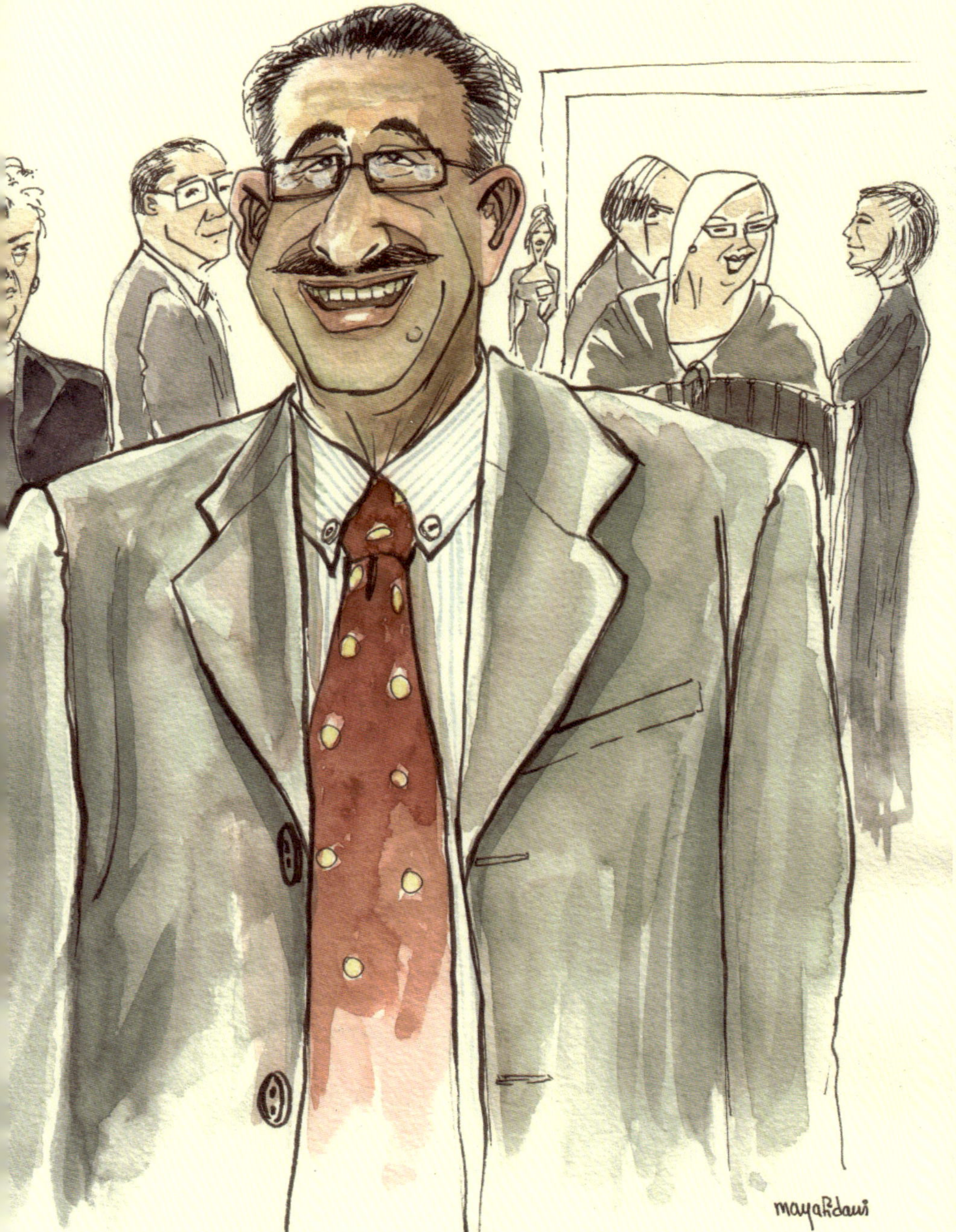
mayafidawi

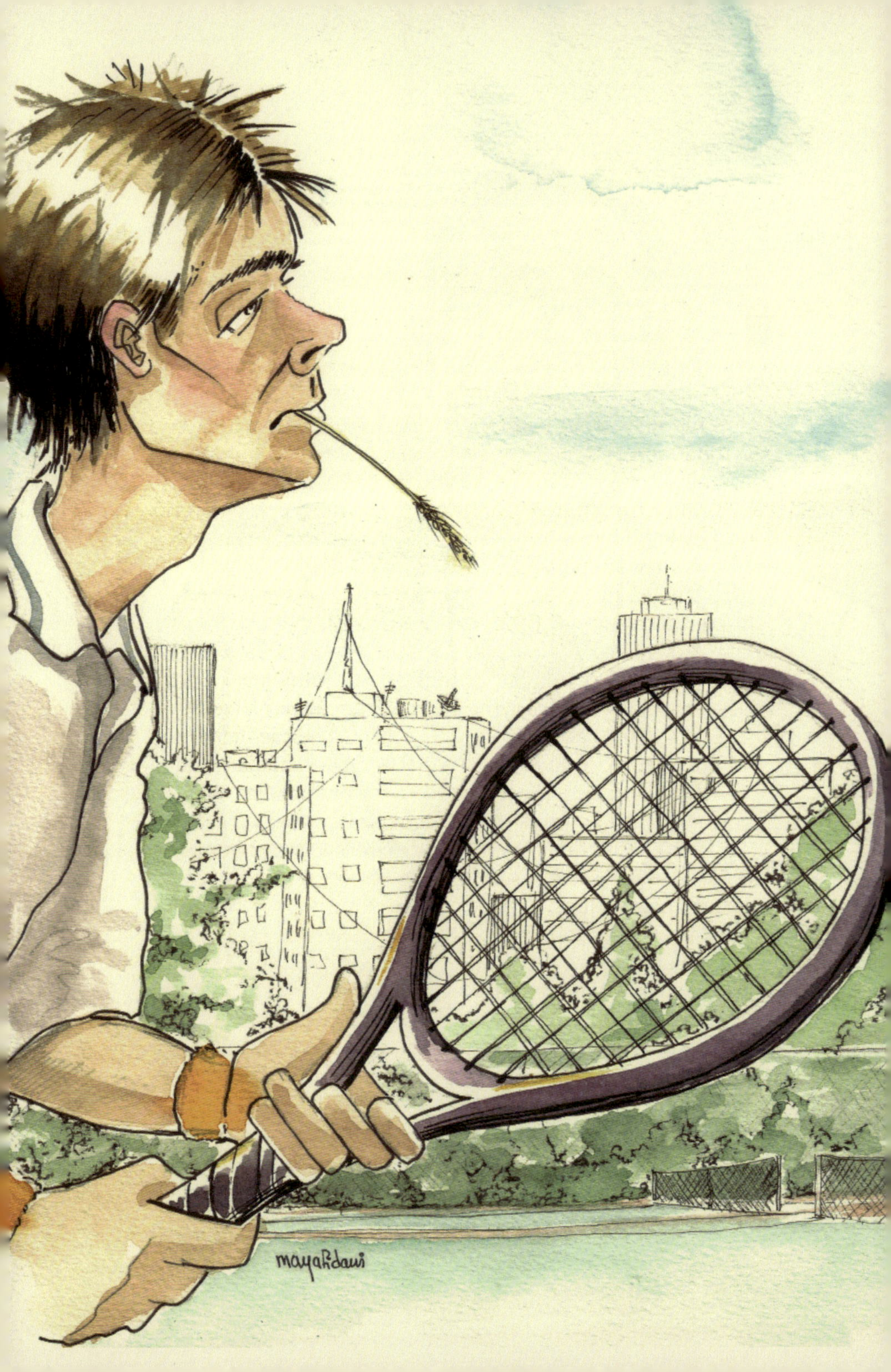

Tennis Player

Tennis player is what happens when a hormone imbalance occurs during fertilization. The result is more testosterone than brain cells. The grandson of a hardworking émigré who left Lebanon to earn a fortune in Brazil, Mazen was pushed and bullied by his father to "get the education your grandfather and I could not have" and so somewhere in his past he managed to get a few 'A' levels from an international school in London, a degree from a similar institution in Zurich and a Ph.D. from an obscure college in Idaho. The fact that all his alma maters now have libraries and sports centers bearing his family name is a mere coincidence. The family's money comes from making the world's finest ball bearings. His father gave him the title Senior Assistant Vice President. In reality he does nothing. At the office, he spends all day playing a computer game in which he bombs Third World countries or plays one of the card games on his computer which he admits to finding "a bit difficult". Mazen spends his summers doing the rounds of Lebanon's beach clubs, where the sight of his Porsche in the parking lots is enough to make most girls turn around and go elsewhere. In winter he gets rid of his excess energy by playing tennis with his father's clients. Honed by his hours of coaching in Idaho, he humiliates them on court, serving aces and top spin returns to their backhand sides that nearly bounce over the back-netting. There wasn't much else to do on the campus once he had his Ph. D in the bag. He wonders why the company cannot get any new accounts.

Sushi Waitress

The instructions were quite specific. If Anna wanted the job in Ramzi's new Japanese restaurant, the first step was that she should forget she was born in Manila. From now on she was Japanese. She didn't have to change her name but she did have to make drastic alterations to her appearance. Ramzi would supply the names and types of appropriate make-up, as well as a set of 8x6 color photos showing the look she had to copy and the hairstyle she must follow.

The uniform, complete with small bustle, would be provided and she must also develop two more assets a Japanese shuffle-walk (Ramzi had been very impressed by the authenticity this had lent to a New York sushi bar he visited) and a high-pitched but discreet giggle (an "essential" that owed more to bad Hollywood movies than to Japan).

However, there was one aspect of her natural Filipina aggression that would stand her in good stead. Restaurant economics depended partly on how many times the same table could be filled with diners over a lunch or dinner session. No one should be allowed to sit in front of an empty sushi board. Empty tables encourage patrons to leave. Anna was particularly enthusiastic about this and often removed the board after the last piece of tuna had left the board but before it hit the mouth. Ramzi was proud of her although he'd been a little worried at first when he discovered she was asking if customers wanted ice with their saki.

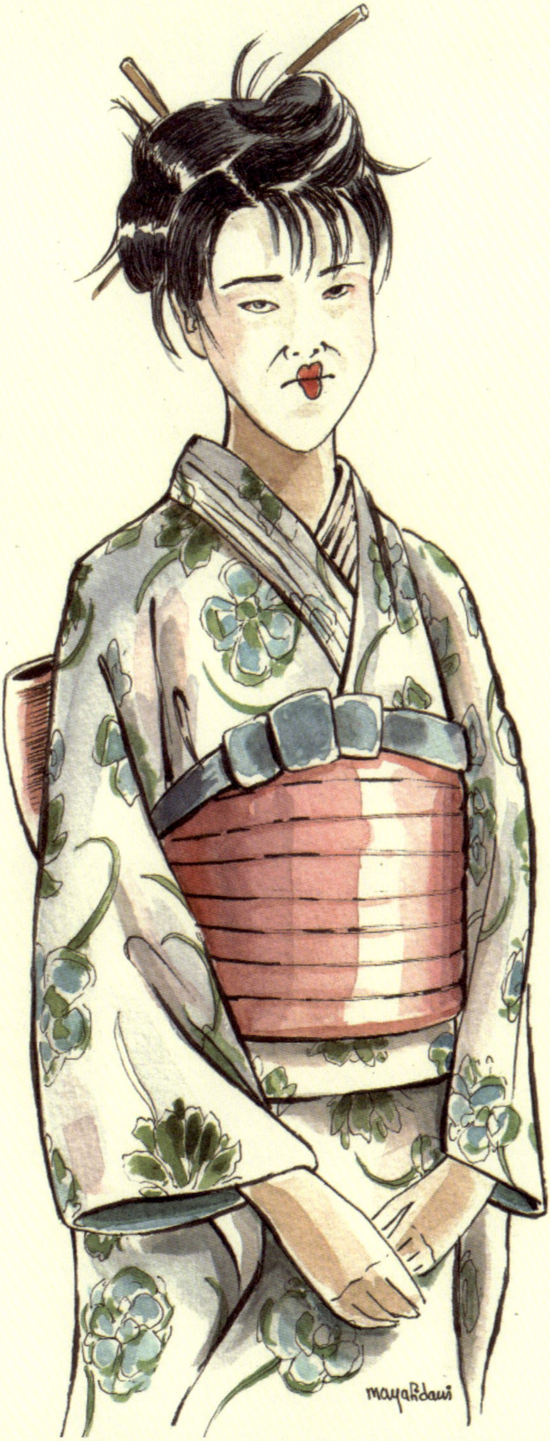

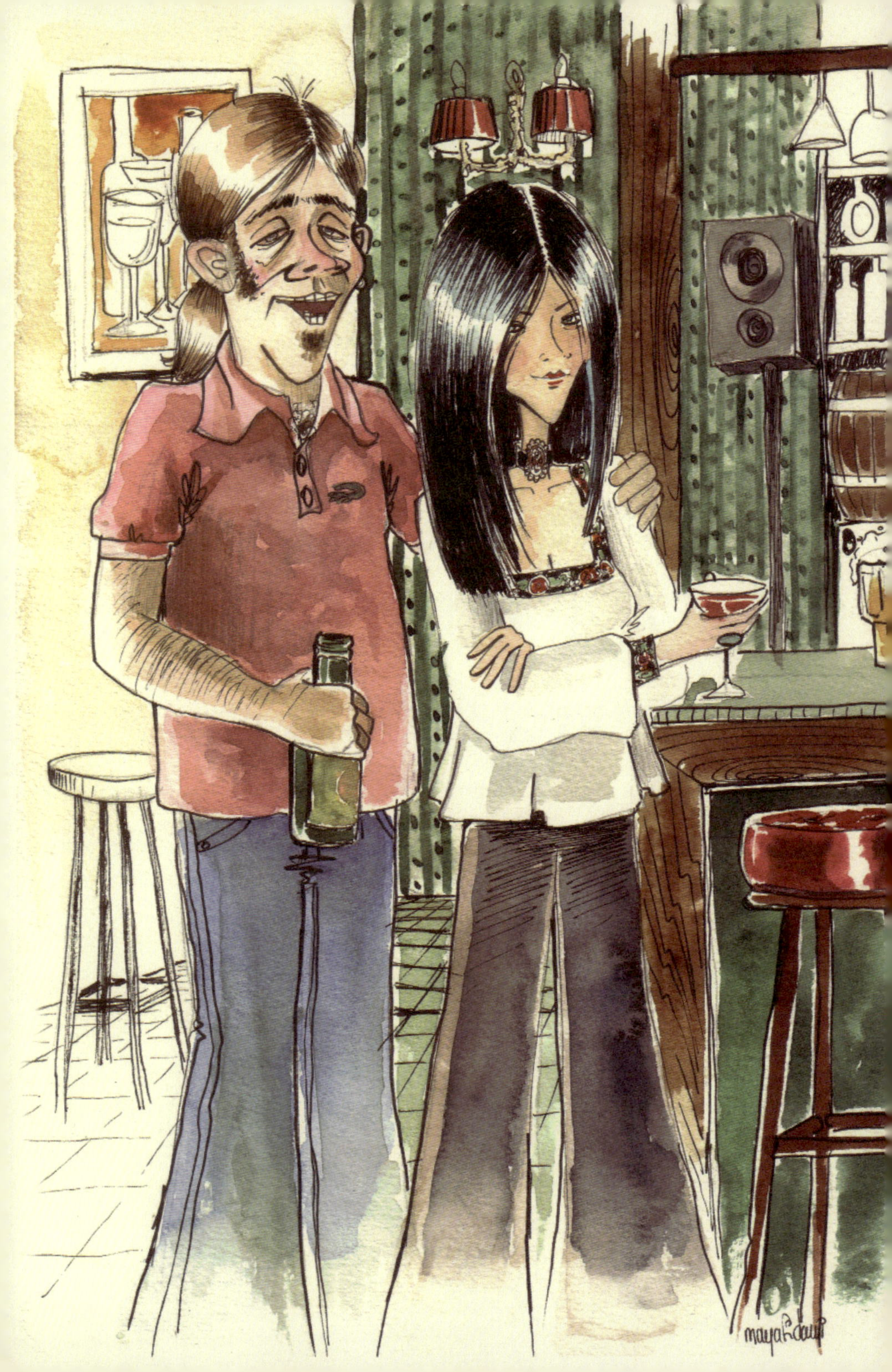

Foreign Bar Owner

Foreign bar owner owns an Irish-techno pub. He is originally from South London and his wife Hiam is from Zalka. She is his third. The first was Dawn from Romford. That didn't last long. She didn't want to travel to "all them foreign places". It was then that he realized that he was too big for England. He went to Thailand and meet Mai Tai, winner of the Miss Pataya wet T-shirt competition. He had his own bar by then, but had to skip the country after the vice squad started making inquiries. Then it was Dubai, where he ran another pub, "The Sinking Dhow". Ironically it actually did sink when his partner ran off with the takings and his air stewardess girlfriend and he had to scuttle it in the creek to claim on the insurance. It was then he thought of Beirut, where his cousin Derek was running the Startled Starfish in Mansourieh. They worked together for a few months but he wanted a better clientele and went into partnership with Georges and opened Paddy's House of Acid on Monot, where he plays Rod Stewart and the Rolling Stones ("proper music"). That is where he met Hiam who was finishing her studies in marketing at Lebanese Colorado College in Dekwaneh. Is he happy? He's loving it. He can't speak Arabic but figures that *yalla* and *bookra* are all one needs to get by.

Bohemian Feminist

Bohemian feminist is a painter. She lives in a tumbledown house in Gemmayzeh. She is divorced after a disastrous marriage to Walid, a neurosurgeon, who now lives in Fresno, California. He got his freedom to live with Brad; she got a lump sum and a free annual CAT scan. Liberated, she now hangs out with Beirut's artistic diaspora and has made a name for herself among Lebanon's intellectual elite. She did however feel she had sold out when she agreed to be photographed with the first lady, but her parents were pleased (always important). She is casually involved with Marco, an Italian archaeologist. She sometimes gets irritated that he disappears for days on end but to complain would fly in the face of her feminist creed. She dresses in black and sits at Rawda sipping a nargeileh. As for the rest of her family, she still has a soft spot for her mother whom she doesn't blame for marrying her misogynist father. Her brother is rotting in an African jail for trying to overthrow the president and her father who thinks both his kids are mad, has been reduced to a shambling wreck wandering around the house asking where he went wrong. She gives a course in "art and politics" at AUB but despairs at the type of girls that attend her classes. They nod their heads and appear to take in what she says, but then they all enter the Miss Lebanon contest.

COLOR INTERVENT
OIL ON CANVAS.
100 X 180
VAIN
OIL ON CANVAS
3500 USD

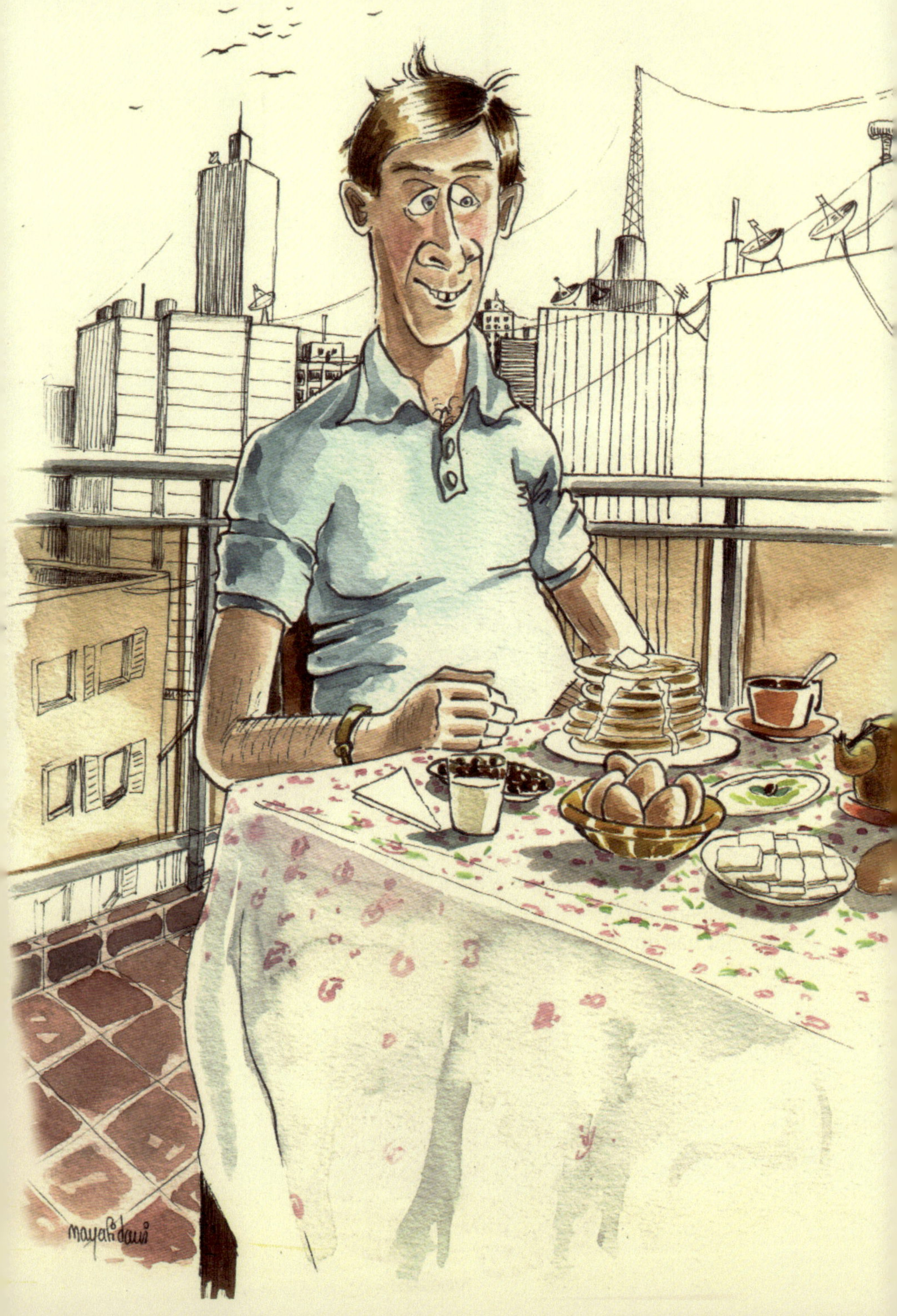
mayaldaui

Fils à Papa

Fils à papa is 32 and still lives at home. Mummy does his laundry and ironing and brings him a cup of Cocoa in the morning. He favors blue button-down shirts, jeans (ironed) and loafers. On his right wrist is the obligatory bit of gold (a gift). He works in insurance, but spends most of his day on the phone to his girlfriend arguing with her about the one evening a week he plays poker with his friends. His loves in life are (in order of importance) his car, his dog, and his family. His girlfriend comes somewhere behind his electronic organ and his shotgun, which now sits behind the door because of the hunting ban. He claims to love 'nature', but after a few whiskies has been known to sit on his balcony and blast away at anything that flies. His mother tells him to stop, but he just tells her to make him another Picon sandwich (toasted). He and his dad bond by discussing what cars they will buy next year. In the meantime his mother hopes he will meet a nice girl and get married. What she doesn't know, is that every girl he meets is compared to her. And why shouldn't she be? When he does leave home he will have to live with someone who cleans and irons his clothes and cooks for him like his mother has done all his life.

Golfer

His biggest handicap was that he was a lousy golfer but, hell, the sport was only a part of being a member of the "club". He had watched the US Masters often enough on cable to know all the right gestures and Boutros even sported the plus-fours and cap that made him the most dignified player on the course. Regular appearances over the years - usually midweek mornings when there were few other people about - had eventually earned him instant recognition by all the members and staff - as well as a place on the committee. And that meant having his name on a plaque on the clubhouse wall, which he read, even if no one else did, every time he entered the clubhouse. It was also the only place where the barman knew exactly how he liked his gin and tonic.

Out on the course, Boutros had the preliminary ritual off to perfection. Pluck a few blades of grass and throw them into the air to test the speed and direction of the wind. That there was scarcely ever any wind didn't matter. If it was good enough for the US pros, it was good enough for Boutros. Bending his knees to check which way the ball would break on a green was a little difficult these days with the onset of age so he checked them standing up but just as thoughtfully.

At competition time, he usually pleaded that organizational and administrative duties as a committee member prevented him from taking part personally. But Boutros finally triumphed. He was awarded the prize for the longest-serving member never to have won a trophy.

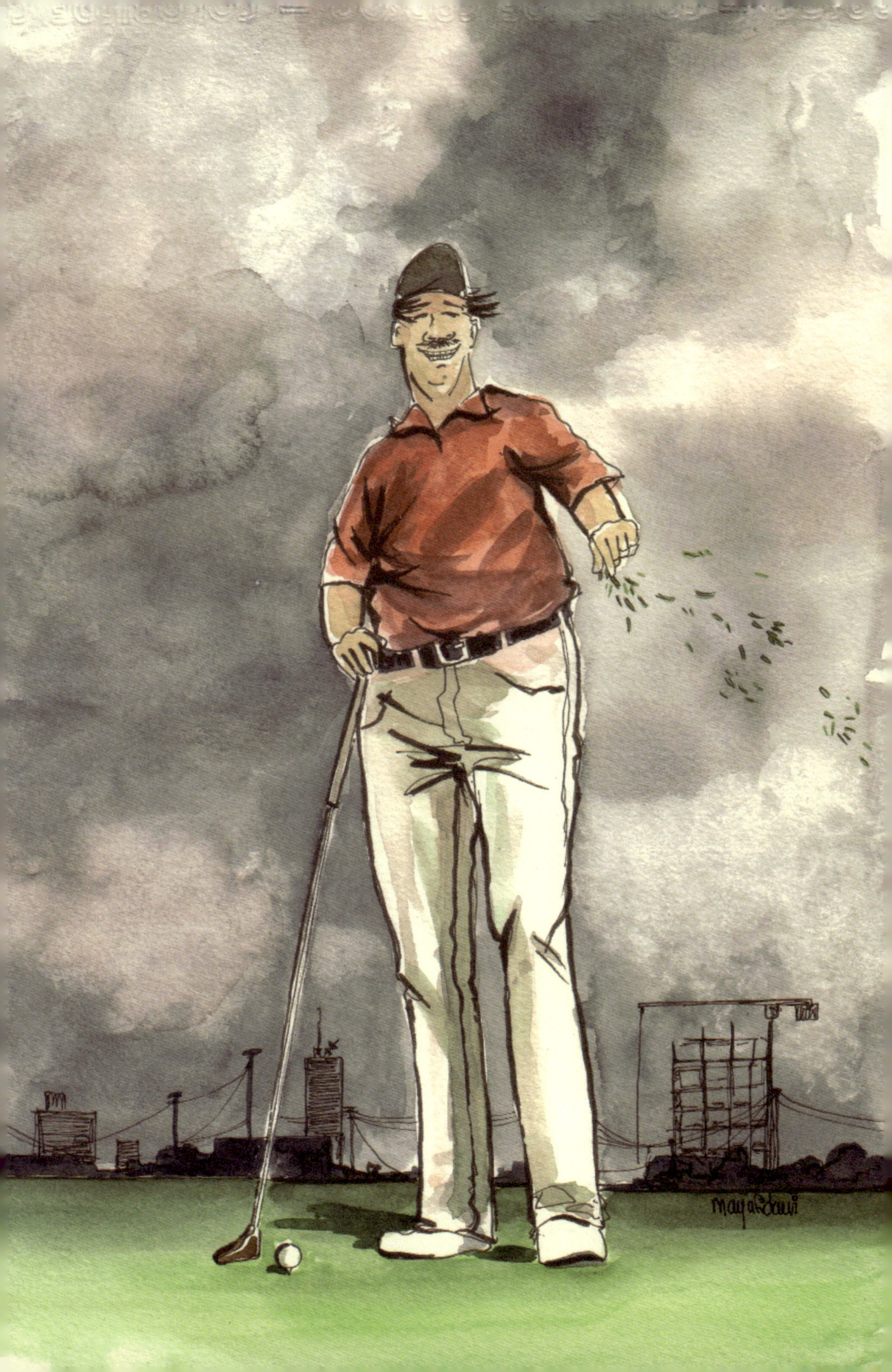

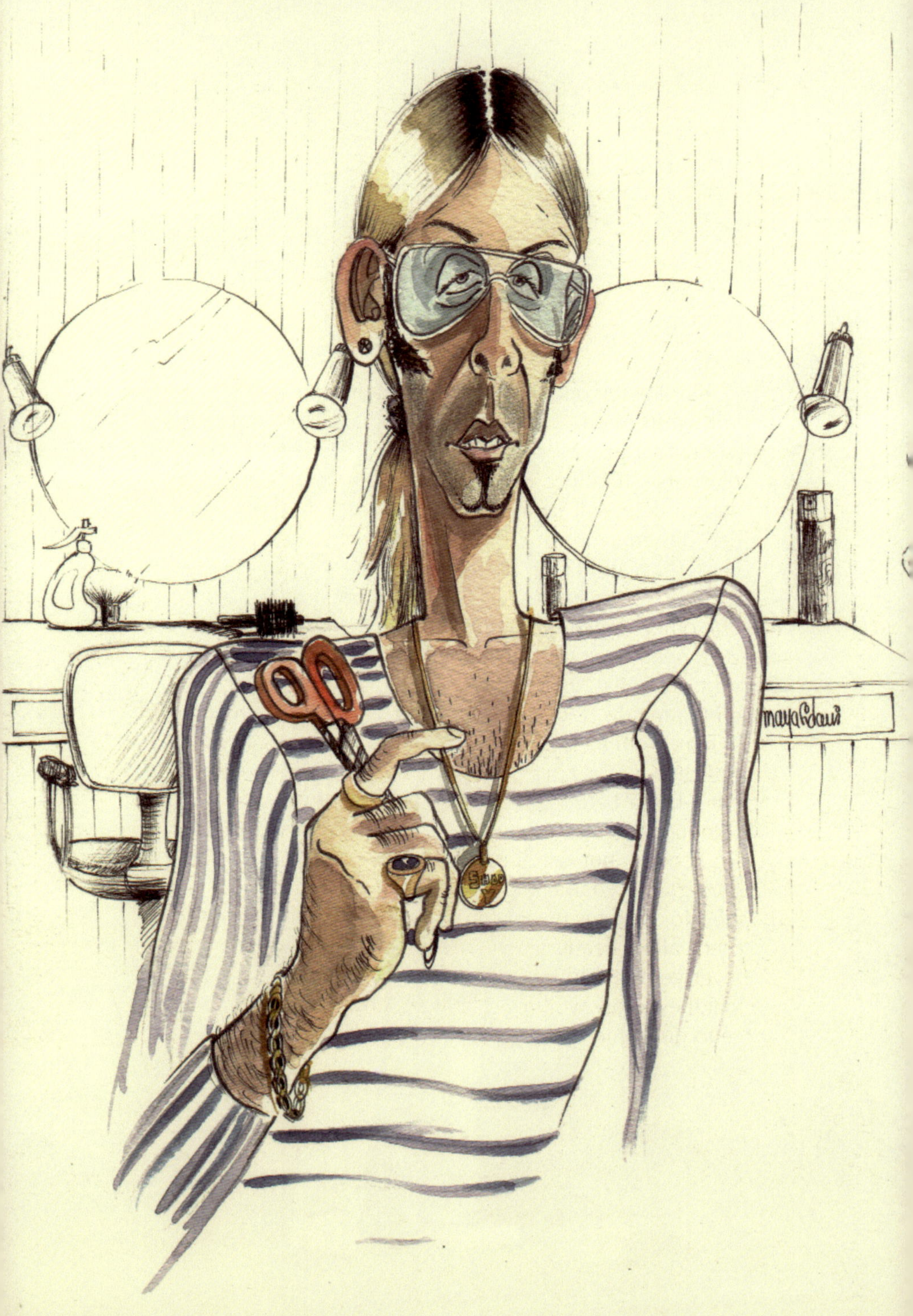

Society Hairdresser

Society hairdresser opened his own salon after a five year apprenticeship with Fuad "Foofoo" Khalil, arguably the greatest coiffeur in the history of Verdun. When he left, there was, of course, a falling out. "Foofoo" was devastated when Mrs. Tabara defected, taking the entire Thursday dining club with her. But he is not sorry. He knew Foofoo would get like that. He lives with his mother and a Siamese cat in Tallet el Khayyat, but is always on call. Mrs. Tabara had a surprise guest the other week and did not come out of her room until he had stopped chatting with the lovely salesman at Zara and traveled all the way to Ramlet el Baida, where he was let in through the maid's door to work his magic. That is why they all love him. Nothing is ever too much trouble. He understands that their hair is their lives. Husbands and children can be controlled but a bad hair day in front of photographer from Look! No, no. It is just too much. Of course he has thought of going to London, but last time he was there they attacked him for wearing a fur coat, a gift from Pussy Hamdan. *C'était très sauvage.* No, Beirut is where he should be, next to his beloved customers, all so beautiful, all so very unhappy. He of course will never get married but he has 30 wives who love him, a man that they know will never let them down. That is why he is there to put some bounce in their lives.

Secretary

For loyalty and devotion Mona could not be faulted. She'd been with the medium-size electrical company for nearly 20 years and for the past five had been the chairman's private secretary. She had seen him groom his three sons to run the day-to-day business and maneuver himself into a position where his only functions were to monitor the firm's finances daily and approve major decisions. After meeting his wife several times at company functions, Mona was a good enough judge of her taste to buy his birthday presents for her and was trusted enough to take calls and make appointments well, dates really with his very special friend in Ramlet el Bayda.

She's also become a practiced and accomplished exponent of being economical with the truth. And just to make sure she was consistent with her story to all callers she kept two diaries, one in a locked drawer only for her eyes and those of the boss, the other detailing the reasons given on any given day why he was not available.

As a last resort to persistent callers, Mona perfected a charming manner of saying she didn't know where the boss was and didn't know when he would be returning. And for those who didn't know when to give up, there was always the fallback of "He's traveling tomorrow and won't be back until next month." The inventions, excuses and lies she used all day provided an unexpected bonus in her private life. Her husband didn't dare to use on her any of the lies she trotted out every day.

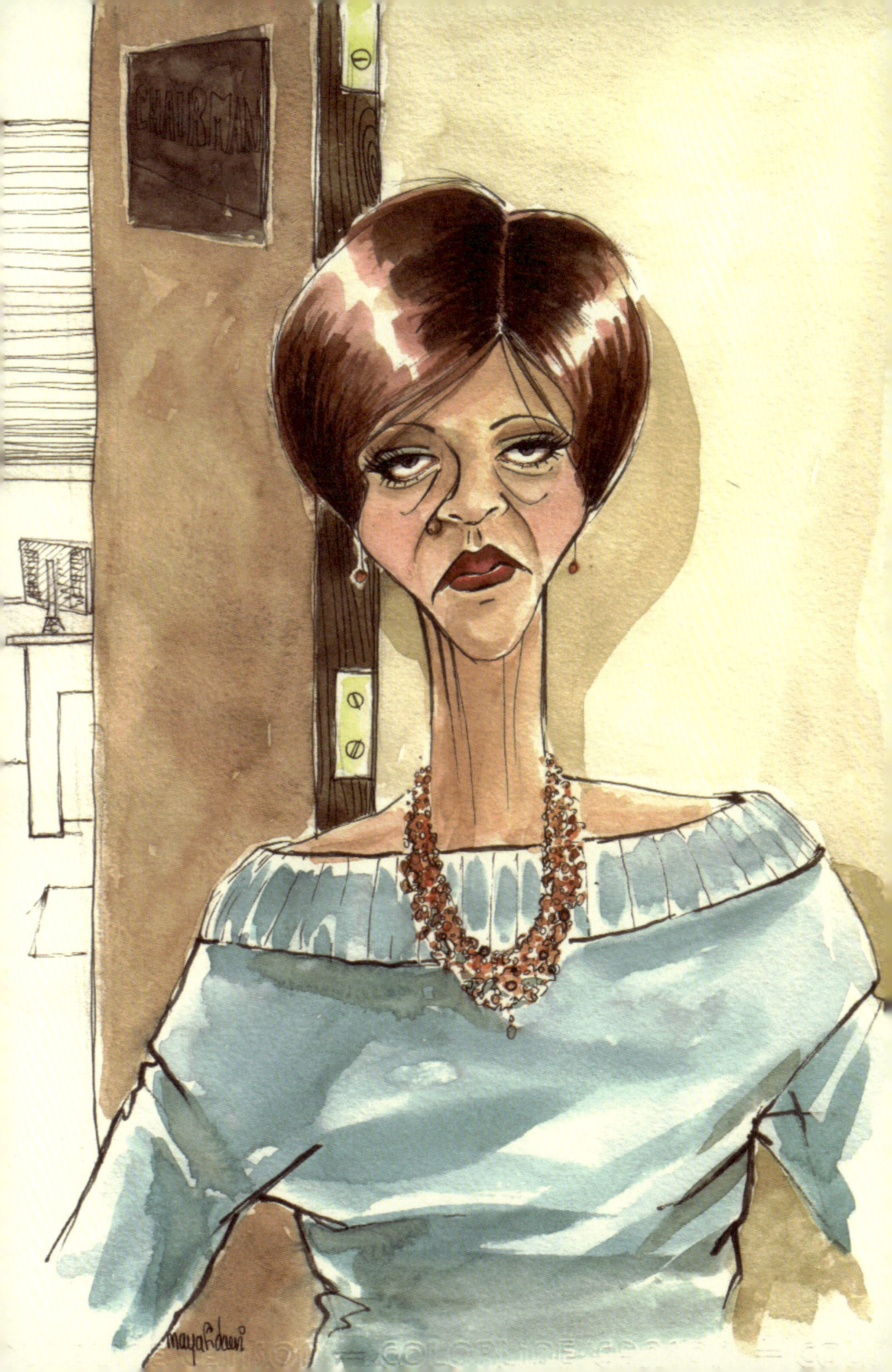
CHAIRMAN

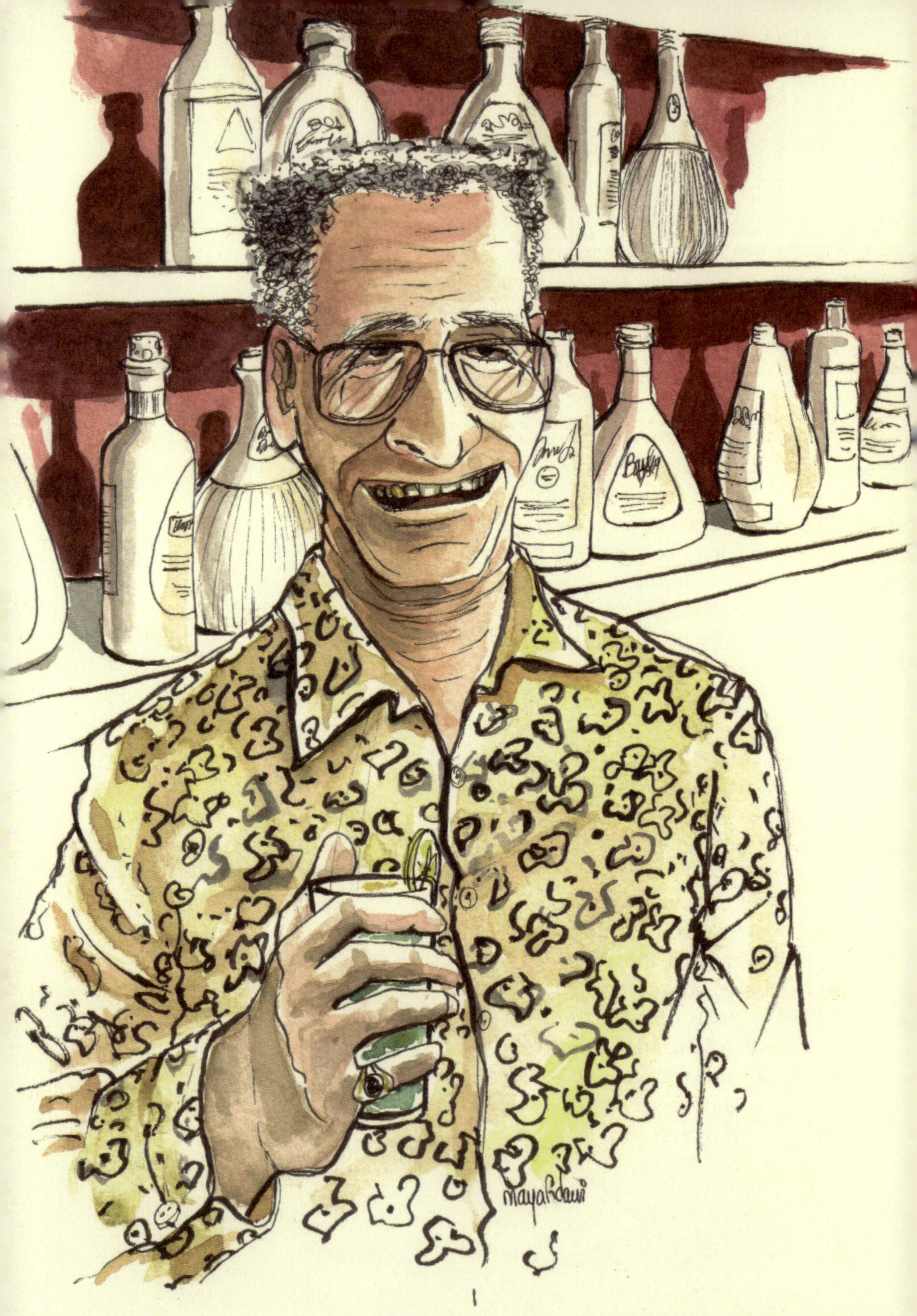

Old Style Barman

Youssef's own view of the hospitality trade was that he was single-handedly responsible for the tourist boom in the 1960s. Although he readily admitted he had no formal training behind the bar, he claimed unrivalled experience and mastery in making cocktails. His guiding light at the beginning of his career behind a bar was never to serve a drink unless he had personally tasted it. True, this conscientiousness and thoughtfulness for his customers had resulted in half a dozen enforced changes of employment when it was suggested that other establishments might better appreciate his individual talents.

At one time he had even tried his luck in Europe, where according to Youssef (now called Joe), he had been in charge of the main bar in a five-star Helsinki hotel. After his return to Beirut three years later he earned the nickname Finnish Joe. The soubriquet was unkindly changed to Joe's finished for a period when his latest move saw him in a grubby bar of doubtful reputation.

Youssef's expanding waistline slowed him down even more than age but the reminiscences, especially to foreigners, of how he had served the rich and the famous were incessant. He also spoke often of the offers he received to help run a ski resort in Switzerland or a beach resort in the Bahamas and it was only family obligations that stopped him from taking them up.

With such assets it was ridiculous he was working for just $350 a month. But at least he never had to pay for his own drinks.

Lebanese Abroad

Lebanese abroad Ibrahim went to America and became Bob. His brothers Ali, Hamad and Farid all became Al, Tony and Frank. Now everyone thinks they are Italian which is kinda cool. Bob and his brothers established a coat hanger manufacturing plant and have all taken American wives, apart from Tony who went home for six weeks and came back with Fatima (now Raquel). Bob loves America. He speaks with a wild American accent and uses words last heard on an episode of Bonanza. But he misses Lebanon. So much so that he sobs whenever his mother calls and tells him what she has cooked that day, reminding him how much he liked her *tabbouleh* when he was growing up. His wife can't understand how, what is essentially a salad, can have such an effect on a grown man. But this is nothing compared to near hysteria generated when he tells his kids Jamal (Jim) and Layla about their roots, especially the wildly exaggerated stories about *Jiddu* Selim and *Teta* Selma. When Bob brings his family to Lebanon for the summer, every two years, he wears stripy polo shirts, shorts and sandals with socks. He takes his family to outdoor mountain restaurants, where he drinks *arak* and gets sentimental, before trying to do the *dabkeh* and nearly breaking his neck. Earlier on in the meal he is asked by at least five cousins to lend them money or sign over plots of land that they convince him they will farm and make him money. He was never this popular when he lived here.

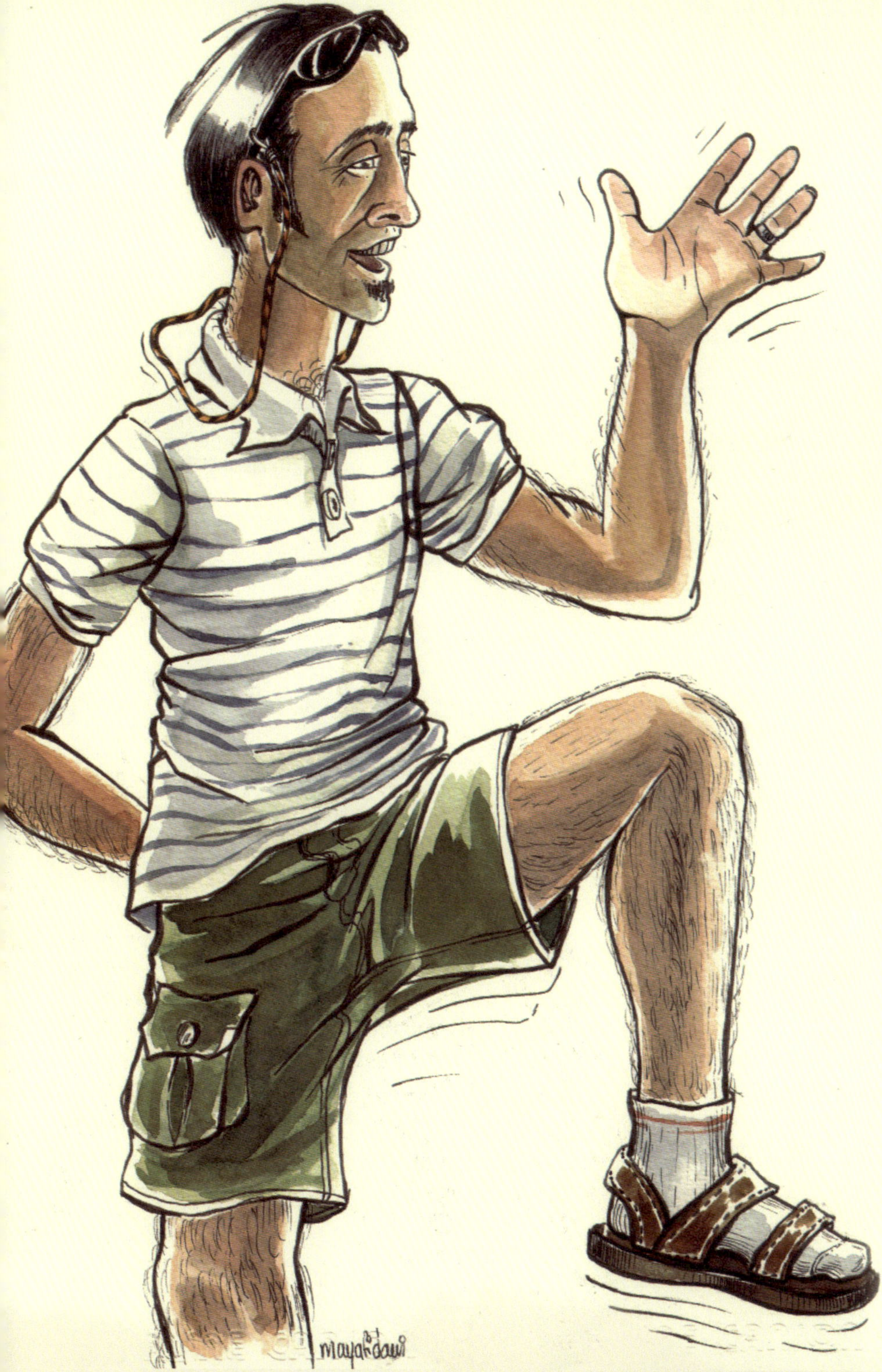

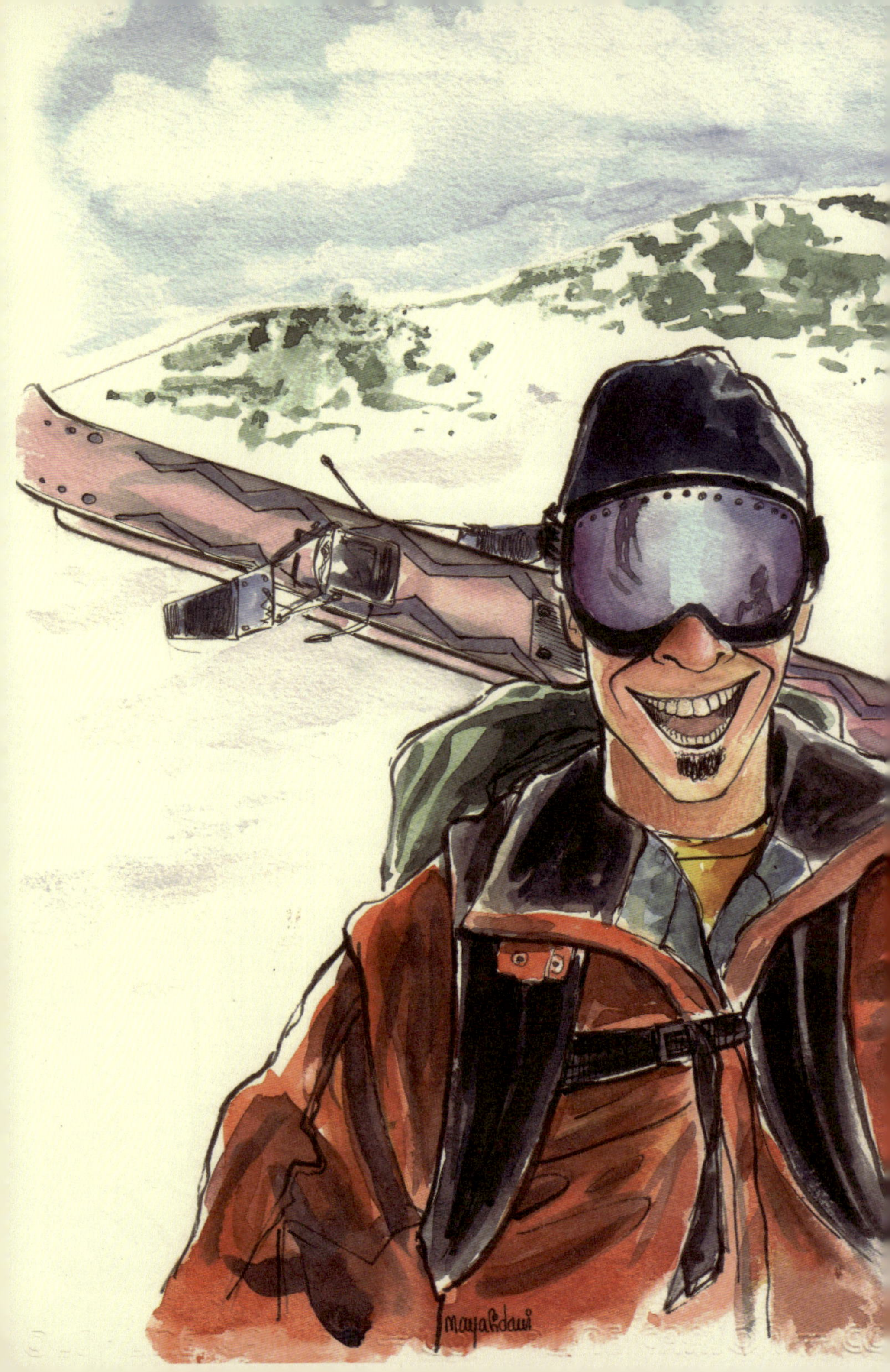

Ski Bum

Naseem had a deal with his dad - he'd work in the family electrical business for nine months a year if he could ski for the rest of the time. And no one on the mountain got better value for a season ticket. Every day he was in line - most of the week he was the line - when the lift opened at 8.30 a.m and he skied till it closed. The seven-year-old Salomons didn't so much fit his feet as feel like an extension of them and his 195 K2s had to be the best maintained in the country. Perfectly waxed and sharp as a razor, they were his passport to freedom and a bigger buzz than any of the still-sleepy partygoers would ever feel.

The unshaven, rugged man-of-the-mountain look may have made him feel the part but the pre-ski exercises and stretching weren't for show. His muscles had to be warm, his legs in tip-top condition. Though his equipment wasn't designed for it, Naseem could slice through deep powder with style and ballet-ski down the pistes forward and backward with the grace of a Bolshoi ballerina. His red one-piece suit was designed for aerodynamic function not fashion, and certainly not to attract admiring glances from girls who spent more time on their make-up than their skiing technique.

Saturdays and Sundays were the worst days when the weekenders transferred their downtown driving habits to the slopes. That was when he shot off piste to go powder skiing and it was where he met Andrea, neck deep in flaky snow...

Security Guard

Saeed couldn't resist a smile of pride every time he adjusted his tie before setting off for a 12-hour shift as "head of day security" for a small publishing house. That's how he saw it though it may have been stretching the definition slightly. He was the only security guard but he was also the first member of his family in living memory to have been required to wear a shirt and tie for his job. Only the unkind would argue that his $275 a month was not really indicative of his status.

He had his own desk just outside the main entrance, two separate sets of forms to fill in one for staff and one for visitors and Saeed was on the frontline for Mr. Karim's security. It was a heavy responsibility. Sure, he was employed to guard the entire premises but the job was much more personal than that. Saeed's gratitude for being plucked from the suburbs into this lofty status ensured that he stood up each time the boss entered or left the premises, only just stopping short of saluting his patron. What luck that Mr. Karim's driver was Saeed's first cousin.

As a bonus he was also receiving a burst of free "education" as he plowed through copies of the publisher's two magazines. It gave him yet more opportunities to impress neighbors in the suburbs with his ever-expanding knowledge. The only clue at work to Saeed's old way of life was the ash-covered area around his overflowing metal ashtray.

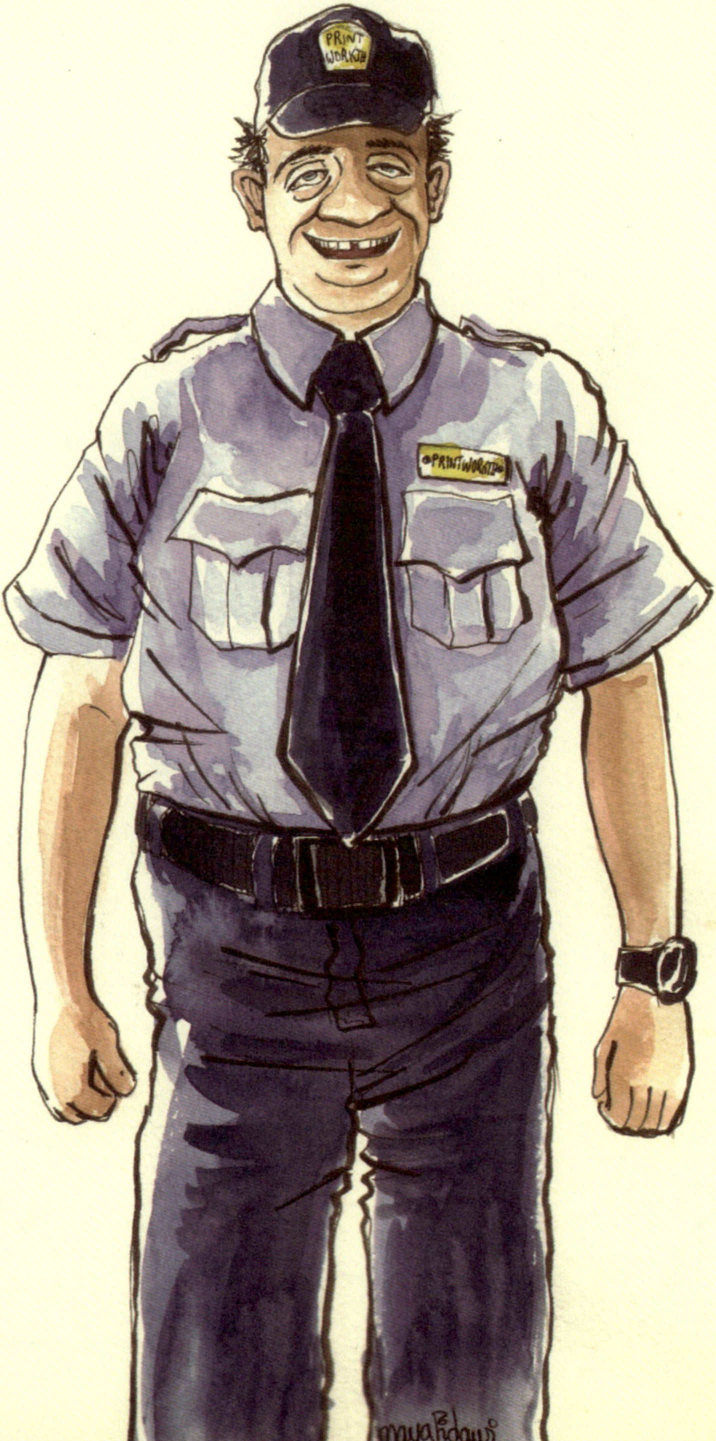
2004

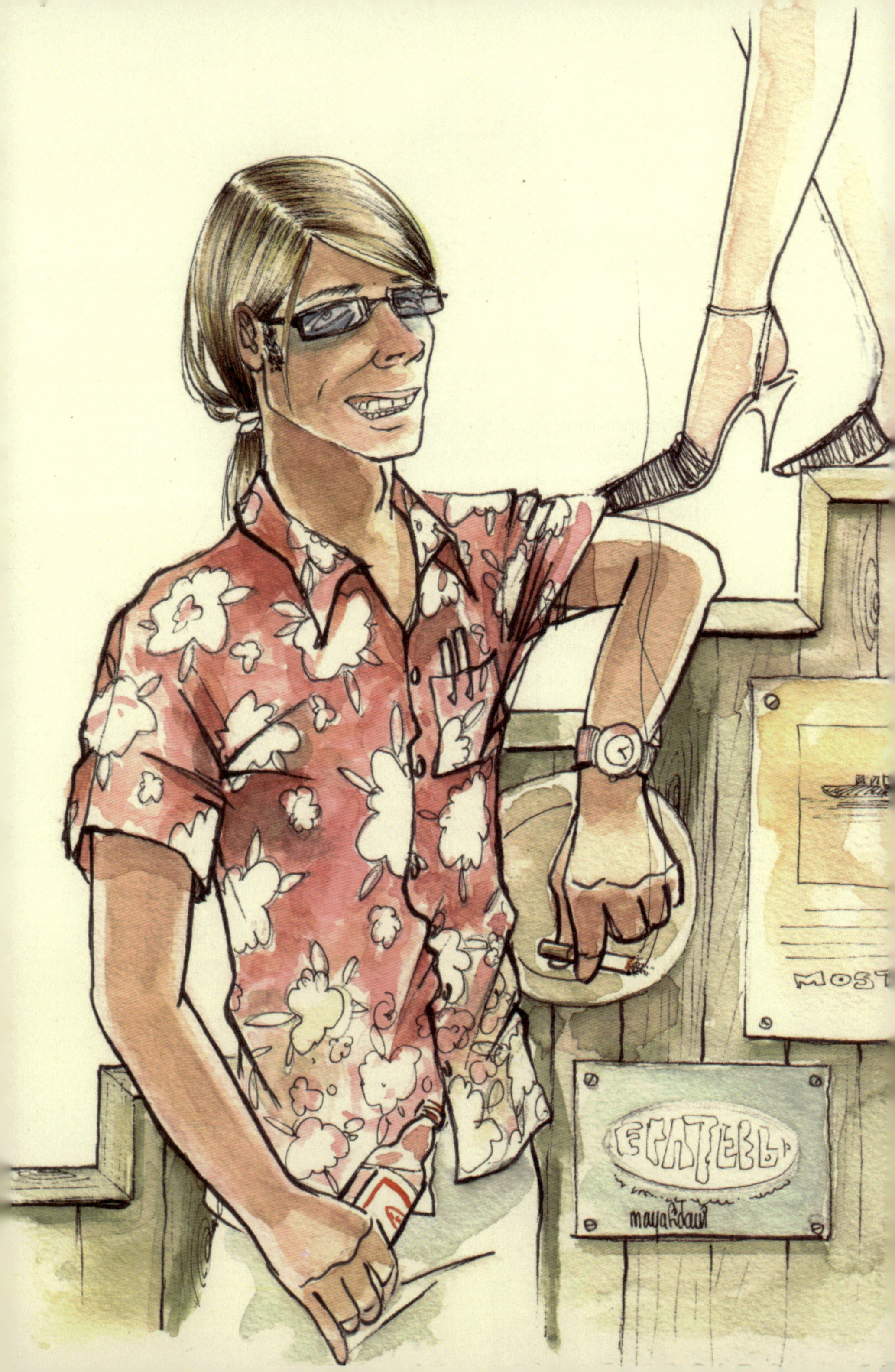
MOST

Foreign Journalist

After three month-long trips to Cairo during summer vacations at Exeter University, Kyle was convinced he'd waltz into a glamorous job as Middle East correspondent for a major British paper. He knew everything about the Middle East, had more than a smattering of Arabic and, of course, he was a brilliant writer. All he needed was an audience. The offer of joining a provincial weekly as a junior reporter was a positive insult. He'd show them all.

Two hours on the Internet convinced him Beirut was the place to be based. It had great newspaper traditions, was at the center of the region - and the women were amazing! With his flowing blond hair - long enough to make him appealing, but tidy and well groomed - the women would be falling over themselves to succumb to his charms.

Kyle's first day on a local publication (just to pay the rent of course until he was recognized internationally) set the style. He would lean over a girl reporter as she sat at her computer, offering his expert help to improve her story and trapping his target with an arm over each shoulder to type a new sentence. At the office's favorite bar after work, it was the same scene - hand on the wall over a girl's shoulder making it easier for her to appreciate his cologne and his personality. But Kyle did have one big effect on the female staff. They all started handing their stories in an hour earlier to be able to leave the office.

Bank Teller

Uncle Hassan had worked for the same bank for 25 years. He had his own office with his name on the door and was given a coffee allowance to entertain clients. Not, of course, that he was allowed to indulge in any banking, like approving loans or overdrafts. But the job had lots of compensations. Until the rules changed, he could leave work at 2pm and help his brother Ahmed run the grocery store. The salary wasn't too high but 14 months salary a year made it more worthwhile and low interest loans helped him become the only member of the family with a new BMW. It was the small one but at least it was new.

After two-and-a-half decade's faithful service, it was only natural for the owner to grant Hassan's request for his nephew Mahmoud to join the bank. Not that he was allowed to work in the same branch. Uncle Hassan's loyalty and integrity were highly regarded, but family - well, that's something else.

A lot of the work had changed too. Hassan had needed authorizing signatures from four supervisors before he was allowed to cash a check as a teller. Now calling up the account on computer and one set of initials was enough. Machines even counted the cash. It was a far cry from the days when Hassan was working in Nabatieh. One Lebanese customer from West Africa, who made a fortune from government contracts after marrying the Gabonese police chief's daughter, walked in to deposit $2 million in cash. Hassan had worked till 3am counting and recounting all the bills.

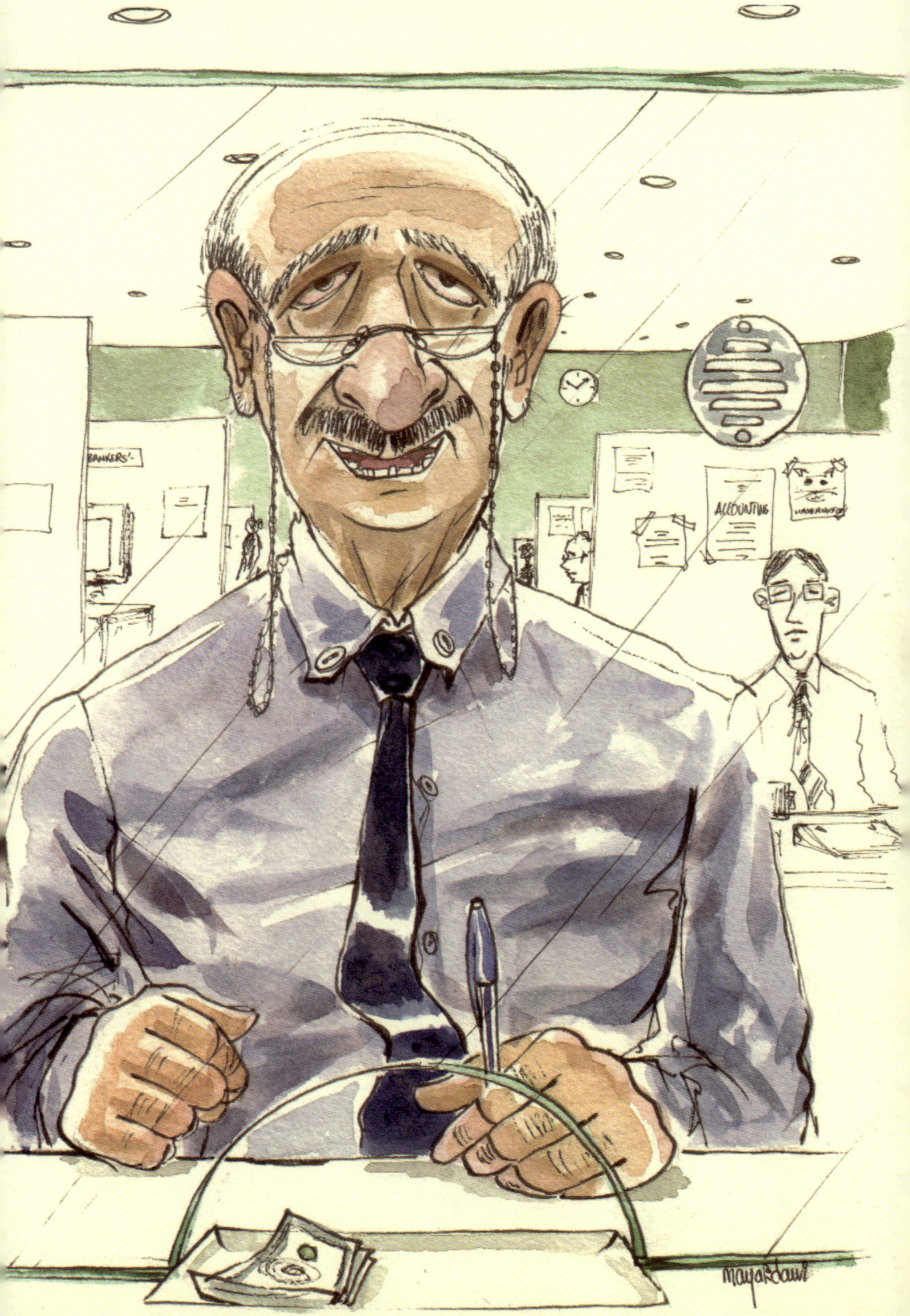
BANKERS'-
ACCOUNTING

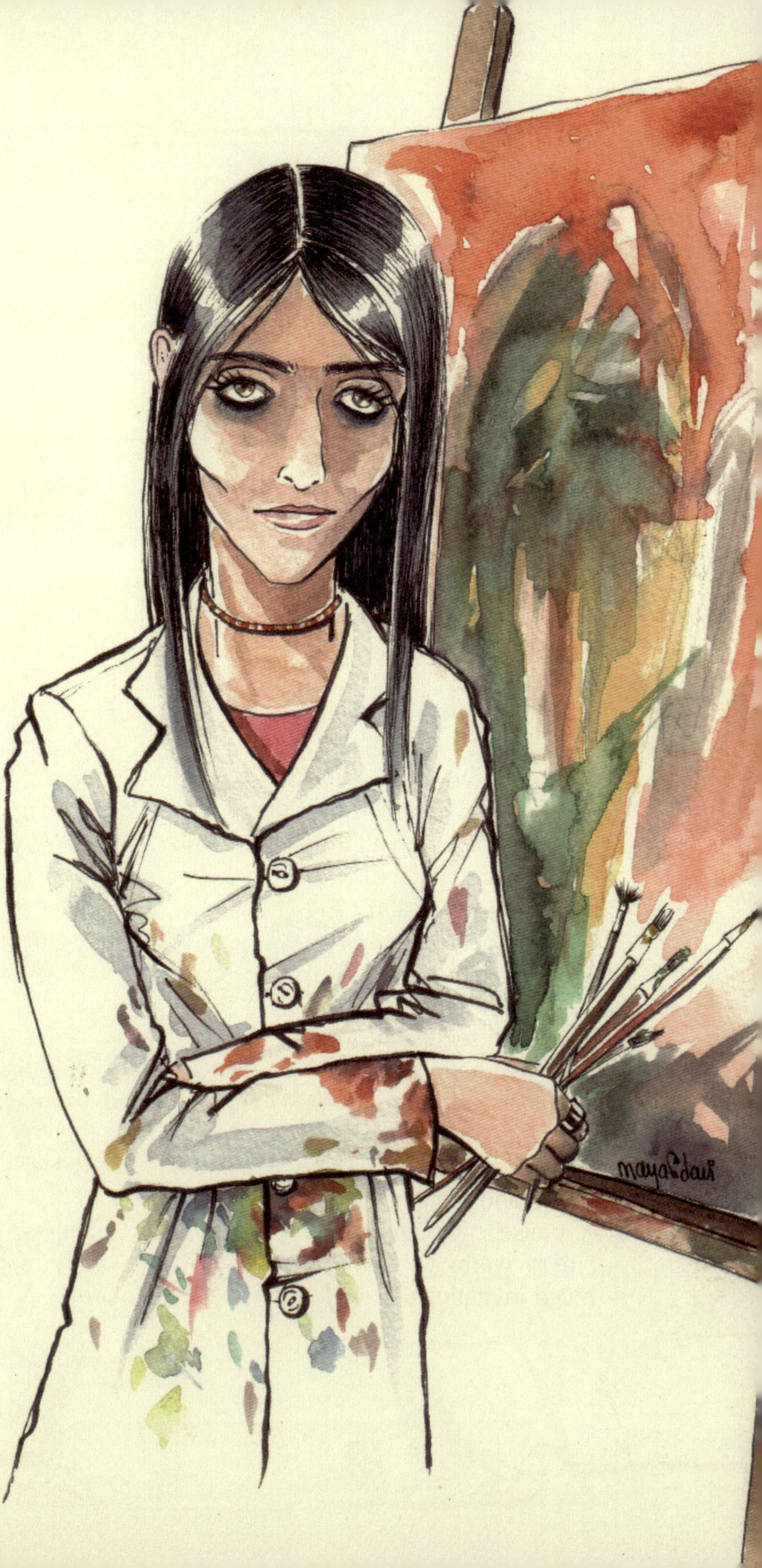

Artist

The intention behind sending Jihane to school in Switzerland was that she should return to Lebanon a refined and polished young lady, with the poise and personality to become the wife of one of three fine young men her parents had picked for her. This silly nonsense of painting would vanish and in its stead would be an appreciation of literature and centuries of other people's art. Madame Fénant unwittingly sabotaged the grand scheme by recognizing, encouraging and developing Jihane's natural gift.

She returned vowing to pursue a love that interested her far more than men and marriage. Jihane also looked the part. She was anorexically thin although it was a lack of interest in food rather than a medical disorder that gave her the waif and stray look. A long black skirt camouflaged her spindly legs and the lowish cut top could easily have been scandalously revealing on a fuller figure. In Jihane's case that peril was averted by having nothing to declare but her talent.

Sent off to seclusion in the countryside with a survival allowance, Jihane painted much but sold little in the first four or five years. In a fit of depression she created an image of a young (and very thin) woman with pained expression as she cut the head off a teddy bear with a pair of scissors. Her friends panicked and thought she was suicidal. The critics loved it and their praise catapulted her prospects. Even Jihane's parents began to warm to having an artist in the family after she received invitations to exhibit in Paris and London.

The Eternal Guest

The eternal guest turns up several hours, or in some cases, days late. This is perfectly acceptable, because he knows that some people never turn up at all. Therefore, by Lebanese standards he is polite. He never worries about calling ahead of time to say he is coming round; this really isn't necessary. Even if his friends are going out when he arrives, he will expect them to drop everything and serve him coffee. If he knows they want him to leave, he will not let on. He knows that if he gets up to go they will sit him back down with the immortal lines "it's still early". This will carry on for several hours. He knows this. When it comes to leaving, he will give himself at least an hour before he really wants to leave. This gives him time to indulge in the time-honored tradition of holding a conversation in the doorway; a decompression chamber if you will. It gets him used to the idea of walking out into Beirut's traffic and smog-filled streets. His hosts play their part. They won't actually let him go even though they want to get to the ten o'clock cinema sitting. For this cultural tableau to be played out to perfection, the elevator door must be held open for the entire duration of the farewell, while irate tenants on the 21st floor bang furiously on their elevator door. The guest then rolls his eyes in that "those are your mad neighbors eh" sort of way, and, suddenly thrust into the role of considerate citizen, will utter a quick "yalla bye" and be on his way.

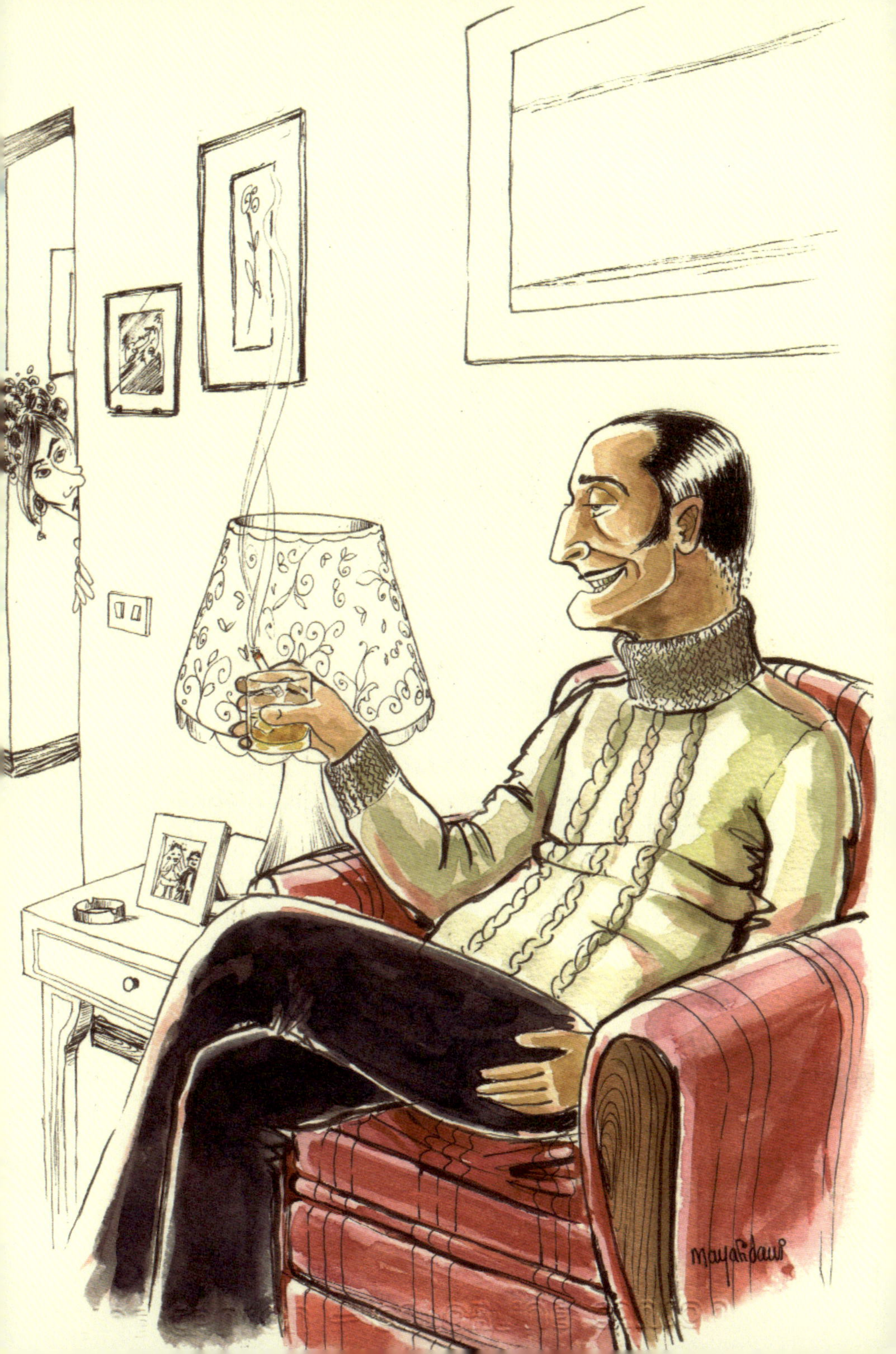

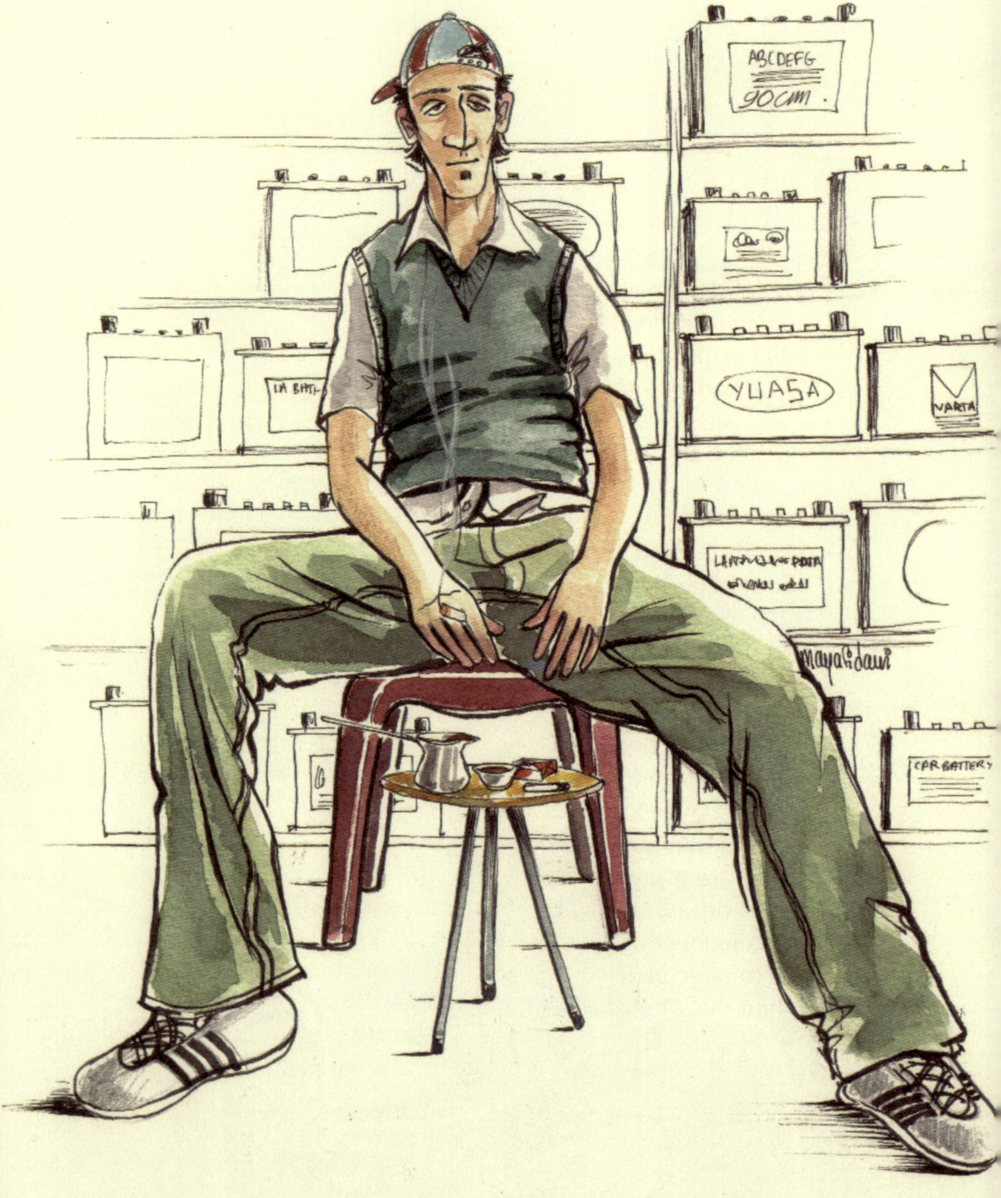
ABCDEFG
90cm
YUASA
VARTA
CAR BATTERY

Non-Job Employee

The non-job employee has, unlike many Lebanese who work very hard to provide for their families, figured out how to work without actually appearing to do anything. Anees arrives at his boss's car battery repair and maintenance shop, pulls up a chair, and sits down for the duration of the working day, sipping coffee and sucking on an endless stream of Marlboros. Only extreme situations, such as a customer actually agreeing to buy a new battery, will give him cause to stand up, but even then it is to tell the garage apprentice to go and get a new battery from the shelf. Other, non-work related incidents are a different matter entirely. Unconsciously, he feels his real job is to offer impromptu mechanical advice in the event of minor accidents. Anees can, if called upon to do so, break-up street scuffles, lend a hand in the shunting of awkwardly parked cars and play the role of ad hoc traffic cop, easing the way for a ministerial motorcade or ambulance. One of his favorite ways to spend the day is to stand around and stare, while someone goes down a manhole, changes a tire or erects a sign. Major road works are a joy and offer him a rare stage to display his knowledge on all matters. These are all tasks that require a degree of engineering and know-how on which he feels he is qualified to offer advice. He lives in the certainty that if it were not for him the whole country wouldn't function.

Fashion Designer

Fashion designer is furious on an almost daily basis. Why Elie Saab and not him? If he has a household name, it is because he is still charging household prices. Yes, there was the fashion show at the Coral Beach where his million sequin wetsuit, the "Scuba Gown" was bought by that lovely Kuwaiti woman and his *Mezze* hat, with real *raqaqat* and *fattouche* embroidered into the design went to the Russian gangster's wife and yes the winner of Miss Campus Personality did wear his fuchsia, jump suit, with the Um Kulthum hologram stitched into the back. Today, he has an appointment with Madam Khoury whose daughter Rana wants something "original" for her wedding cocktail after she marries basketball star Johnny Karam. He has decided to offer her his latest creation: Slam Dunk, a dress made up of sequential basket ball hoops held in place by netting. Johnny will be wearing a "smoking" in his team colors with his name and number on the back. This is what makes him (not Johnny) a star. The people love his originality, his ability to make it all so personal, so divine. He owes it all to his mother, who encouraged him to sew when he was a boy. One day he will show his teachers who mocked his aspirations and his classmates who sneered at the knitting in his desk. Where are they now? All doctors and engineers, while he is one step away from the ultimate commission, designing a dress for the winner of Miss Lebanon. Then he will have truly arrived. Till then, the world will have to wait.

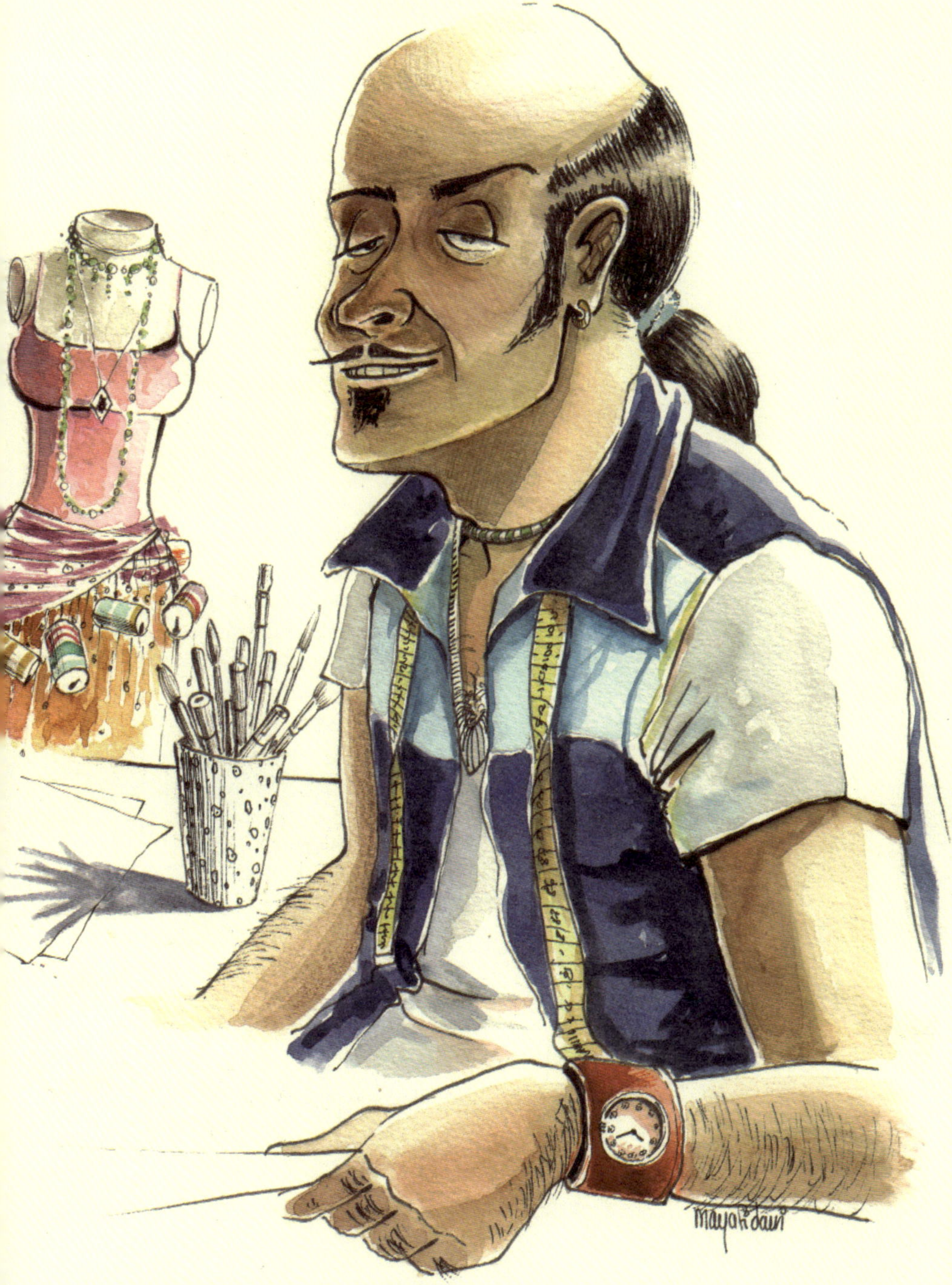

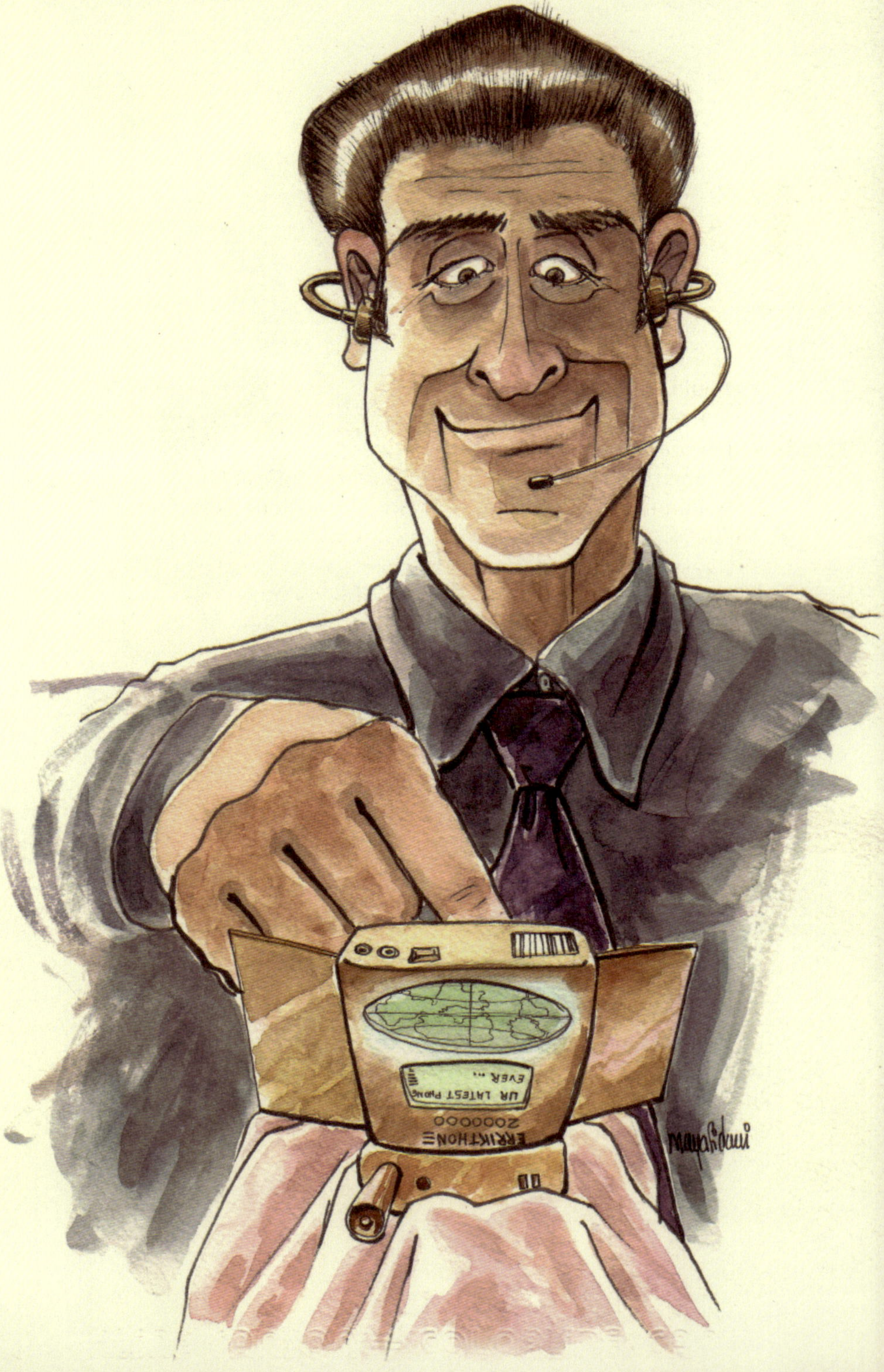
UR LATEST PHONE
EVER ...
200000
ERRIKTHONE

Mobile Phone Fanatic

He could have gone the whole way and parted with $28,000 for a platinum Sony Ericsson but Malek had second thoughts. Money wasn't the problem or even the risk of having it stolen. It was the prospect of having to repeat the hours and hours of programming that had given him 1,143 contacts with internationally coded numbers, addresses, emails, websites and password-protected notes with intimate details of his special friends. Besides, his was probably the only phone in the country to have guides to the subway systems of Paris, London and New York. Not, of course, that he ever rode the subway. Then there were the videos - of his son, his various homes and the naughty one of (allegedly) local singing superstar Haifa Wehbe in various stages of undress.

The wonders of Bluetooth communication enabled him to play poker at the lunch table with his friends and a 512MB memory card provided enough space to have different and elaborate rings not only for family, business and "les intimes" but also for calls coming from different countries. When his phone played the Marseillaise, he knew without looking at it that the Paris office was calling.

Yet one function had been permanently disabled after an uncharacteristic security lapse. The speaking reminder of important events on his agenda had blurted out over breakfast one morning: "Flowers for Wadad and book hotel in Milan." His wife Nadine instantly noted the deficiencies of this wondrous technology. "Your secretary is more discreet than your phone," she said.

Service Driver

Abu Layla must have been the inspiration for the Beirut drivers' definition of hell on earth: To have at the same time an empty service in front, stopping unexpectedly and often (and always in the middle of the road not to lose a place in the traffic), and a full one behind, impatiently intent on delivering its squashed human cargo as fast as possible. It was the frustration of losing his import/export business (or that's what he told every passenger who cared to listen) that pushed Abu Layla. One day, one day, he'd be back on top. Meanwhile $400 at the Sunday morning Service car mart at Cola had secured him a 27-year-old Mercedes 200. The registration papers said it was green, although rust would have been a better description. None of the rear lights worked and the one functioning headlight was enough to spot the raised manhole covers and avoid destroying what was left of the suspension. The only important maintenance for Abu Layla was to keep the horn working.

His first lesson had been: Hoot at everything, no matter which way they seem to be heading. Every LL1,000 counts. He even allowed himself gratuitous honks at shapely legs in a mini-skirt although foreigners, even ugly ones, were more attractive. By carefully avoiding use of the word "service" any stranger was a potential LL5,000 taxi fare. And a friendly rival driver had given him an invaluable tip. Never show passengers you have more than three LL1,000 notes. That way when someone offers a bigger note, you can say with a smile: "Sorry, I don't have any change."

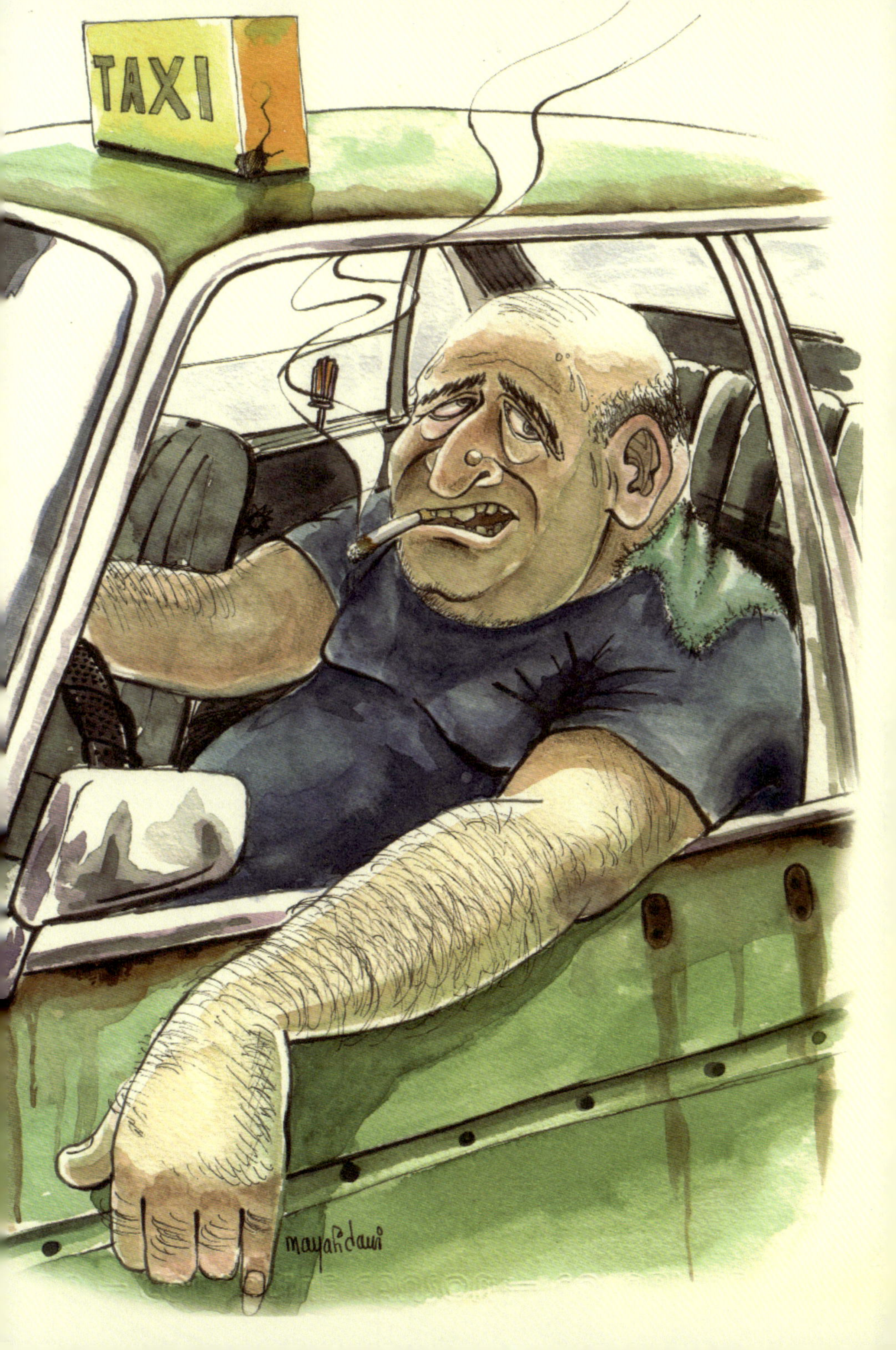
TAXI
mayahdawi

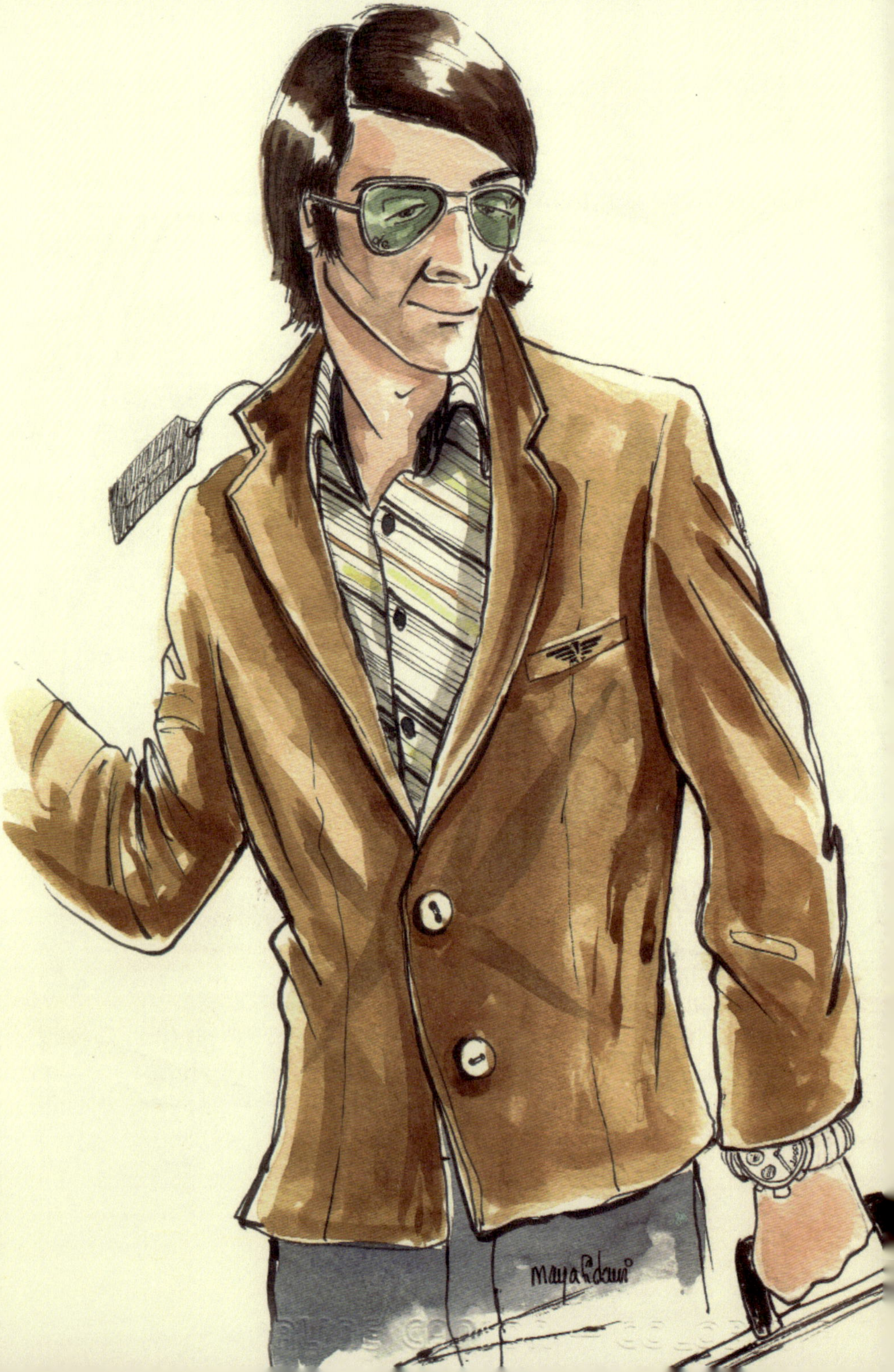

Fashion Victim

Lebanese Fashion Victim is a label man and sartorial assassin, who strikes fear into the hearts of less-hip colleagues and friends. A realist, Rami learnt a long time ago that the Lebanese judge a man by the cut of his suit, the name on his tie, and the weight of his watch. This is why even though he has no taste per se, he is universally held up as a man with impeccable sartorial credentials. Still, every now and then nature throws him a curveball - remember the purple, full-length, sheepskin trench coat? He'd rather not. Officially however, these gaffs are spun as momentary flashes of eccentricity and his friends marvel at his rakish élan. At work, he is a self-styled fashion cop, wandering the open plan office sneering at co-workers who fall short of his standards. With male co-workers, he might grab a tie to inspect the label. He will offer unsolicited advice on the does and don'ts of wearing a belt, perch himself on a desk and hold forth on the correct watch to wear with a "smoking" or how clunky car keys can ruin the cut of a suit. Living a lifestyle predicated on high end accessorizing comes at a price. The red Chelsea boots with Cuban heels, cleaned him out the other month while the "original" horse hide full-length SS overcoat required a personal loan. Still Rami is unmarried and lives at home. When will he realize that clothes do not maketh the man?

Nature Lover

Rabih was the only and lonely child. With his father in Kuwait most of the year and his mother enjoying the better life her husband was working for, there wasn't much choice. At least mother had filled their apartment with plants, though the care and love they received came from the Eritrean maid. He was fascinated by the birth of tightly folded leaves and gazed at them with growing admiration as they opened up into their myriad pure shapes. He was also in awe as she plucked leaves from some plants to eat raw while using others for cooking.

He read up on botany and wildlife from books in the school library since such literature wasn't considered suitable at home for a future civil engineer. In fact, it was on the basis of keeping fit rather than rambling the countryside that he had been allowed to go on 12-kilometer hikes with an adventure group.

On the first day out, he had taken a packed lunch like the rest, but then thought it a waste of time when there were so many edible leaves on the trail. His keen eye could spot lunch from 50 meters and on some hikes he was even saved the trouble of carrying a bottle of water. To the admiration of the occasional ramblers, Rabih knew every spot where there was pure spring water.

The only reason he had a bag was to collect plastic bottles, cigarette packets and soda cans discarded by the unappreciative. Rabih was sad, not angry, when other people discarded more new junk than he collected. One day they'll learn, he thought.

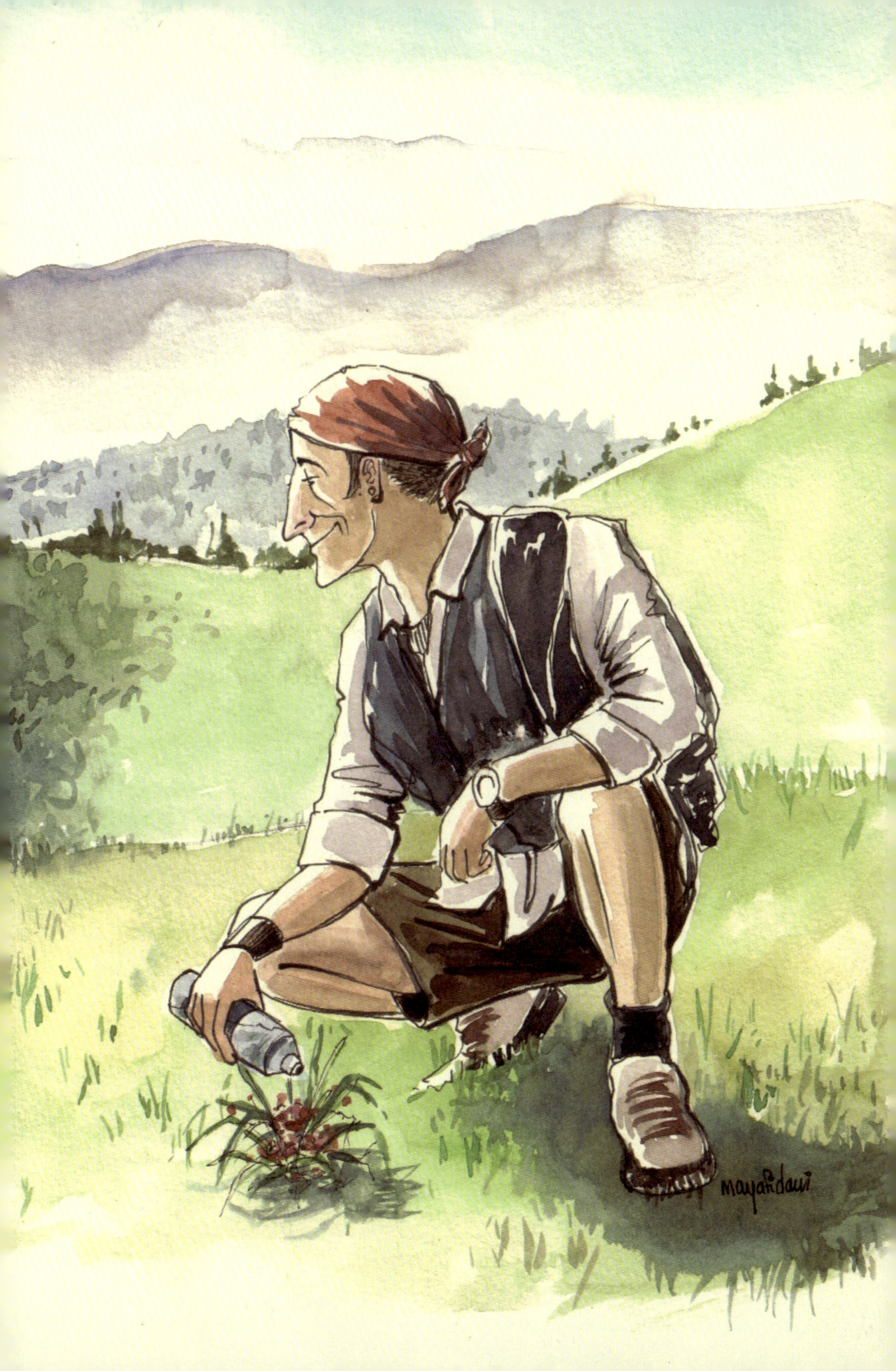

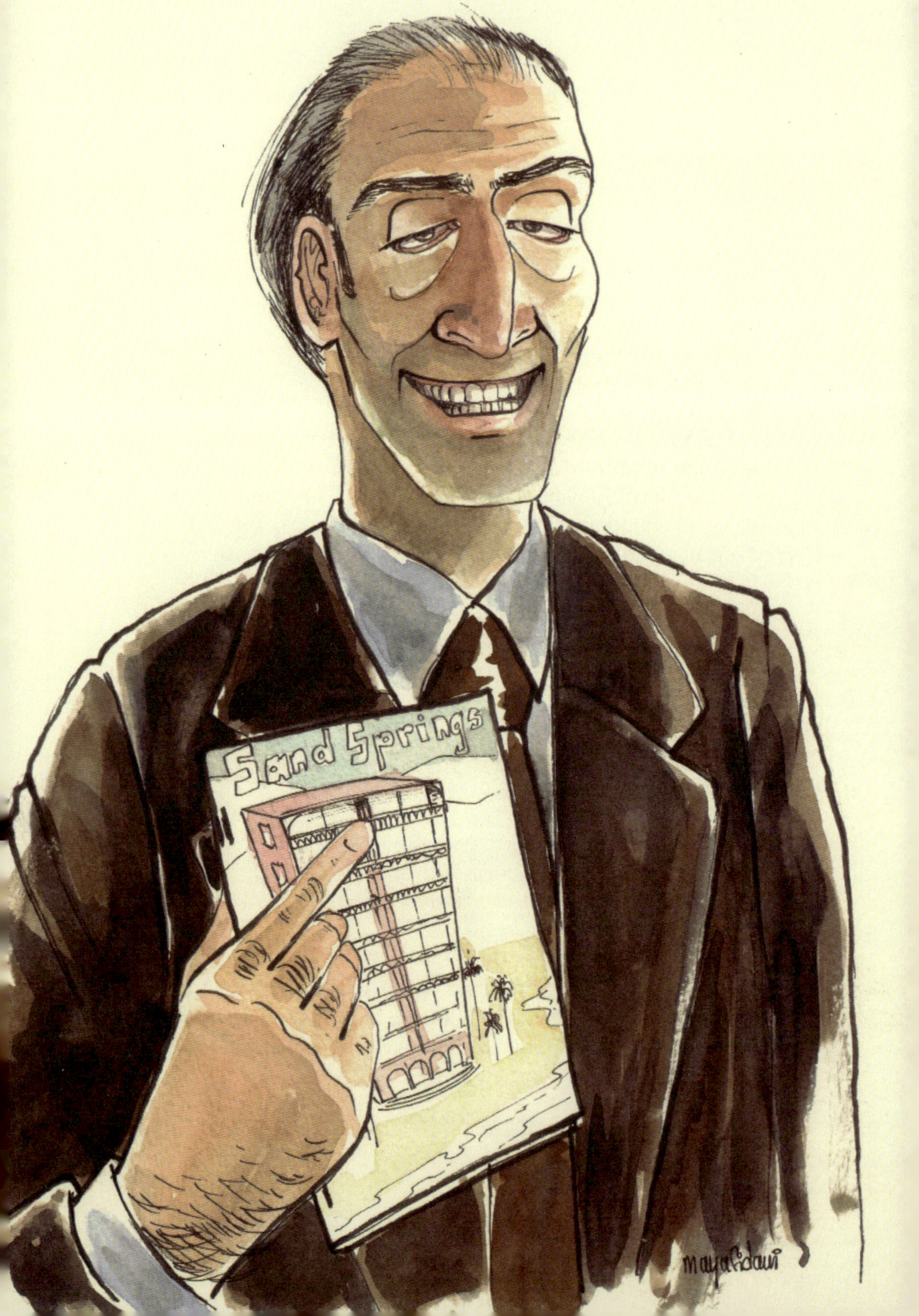
Sand Springs
mayafidawi

Developer

The family conference in Sao Paolo came to a unanimous decision. Salim was assigned the task of turning a 900 square meter land plot on the edge of Beirut into a block of apartments valued at $150k-$200k. Eight on the upper four floors would be set aside for family and the rest would be sold to pay for the whole development. On paper it was foolproof. The numbers all added up. But - and this was a big but - it needed a strong hand to prevent costs from running out of control. And Salim was the obvious choice. He was the only brother living in Lebanon and his background as head of a small marketing company would help in the sales.

There were also several "entirely legitimate" tactics to be employed to make the most for spending the least. The quality of finishing and fittings for the bottom floors would be cheaper than those on top. After all, who was to know? No one would ever view the family's own homes, and the lower floors could still be marketed as being super-super-deluxe. Separate elevators for top and bottom floors would be promoted as providing efficiency, not exclusivity.

The brochures, composed in Salim's more natural French, would be lyrical, painting a picture of idyllic living. Sadly, some of the magic about the sea views was lost in translation, with the English version describing Lebanon's coastline as 200 kilometers of façade. One factor in the slow sales may also have been that you couldn't actually see the Mediterranean until reaching the fifth floor anyway.

Crazy Driver

Abboudi viewed the news that an extra 220 sets of computer-controlled traffic lights were to be installed in Beirut as a challenge. He never stopped at lights anyway, no matter what the color, and even passing through on green gave him a rush of adrenalin because a driver nearly as superb as he is could be passing through the partner set on red. And one-way streets were a very simple concept. He only ever traveled in one direction at a time anyway. It was just that his choice might be the opposite of most other people.

Replacing the exhaust on his BMW had been a masterstroke. It didn't make it go any faster but the throaty roar seems to scare the hell out of everyone else around. And the manual gearbox meant he could press the clutch and accelerator at the same time and, while his neighbors on the road were trying to source the thunderous noise he could dive in front of them.

Driving straight out of junctions without stopping became a point of honor and sometimes he spiced life up by determining to overtake cars alternately on the left and then on the right. Keep them guessing was Abboudi's motto, especially when he deliberately chose the right-hand lane from which to make left turns. Shooting across four lanes of traffic was a good advert for his skills.

Young, alert, with lightning reflexes and perfect control of his car, Abboudi thought perhaps he should have been a rally driver. But the only problem was there were too many rules in rallying.

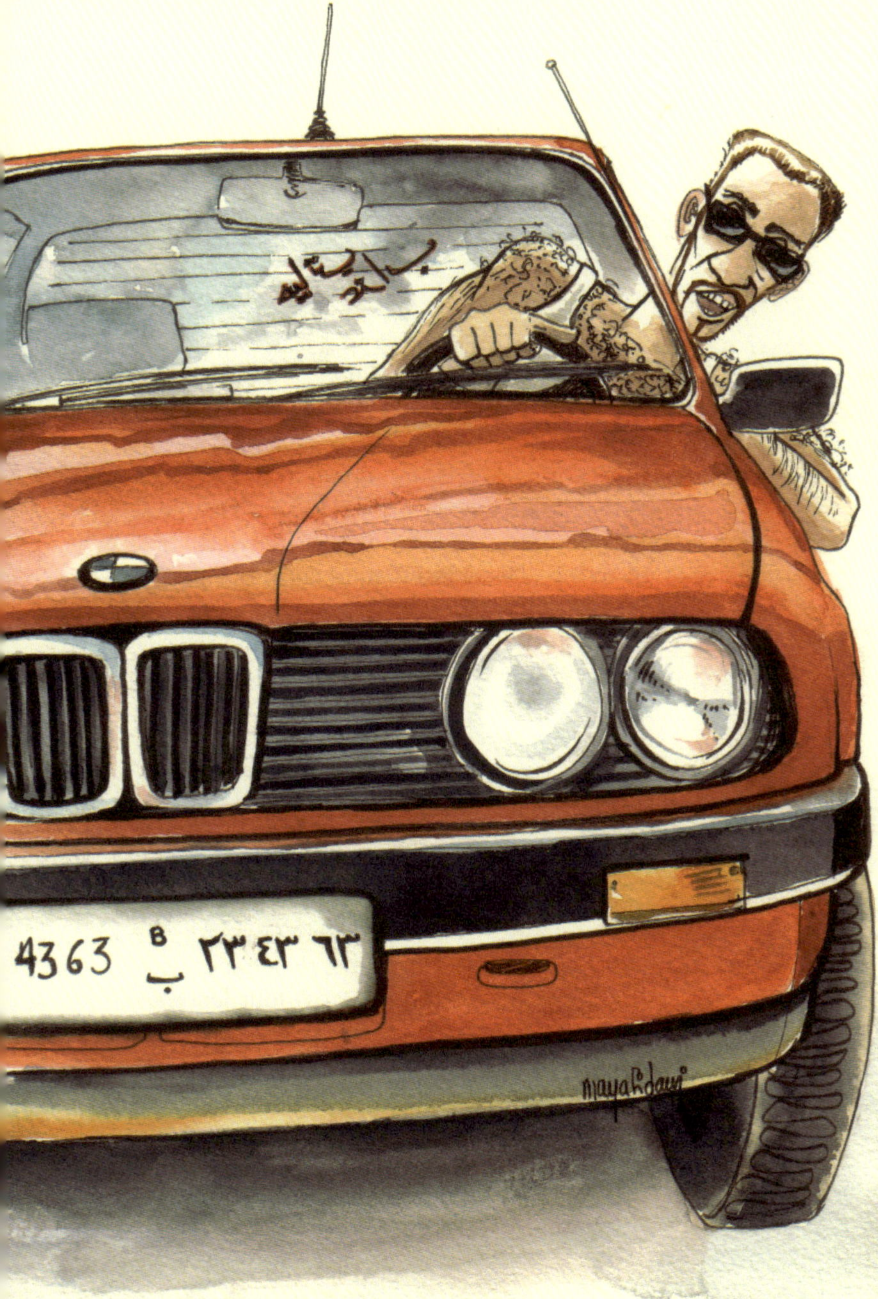

4363 B ب ٢٣ ٤٣ ٦٣

Printing: Dar El-Kotob